Palgrave Science Fiction and Fantasy: A New Canon

Series Editors
Sean Guynes
Independent Scholar
Ann Arbor, USA

Keren Omry
Department of English
University of Haifa
Haifa, Israel

Palgrave Science Fiction and Fantasy: A New Canon provides short introductions to key works of science fiction and fantasy (SFF) speaking to why a text, trilogy, or series matters to SFF as a genre as well as to readers, scholars, and fans. These books aim to serve as a go-to resource for thinking on specific texts and series and for prompting further inquiry. Each book will be less than 30,000 words and structured similarly to facilitate classroom use. Focusing specifically on literature, the books will also address film and TV adaptations of the texts as relevant. Beginning with background and context on the text's place in the field, the author and how this text fits in their oeuvre, and the socio-historical reception of the text, the books will provide an understanding of how students, readers, and scholars can think dynamically about a given text. Each book will describe the major approaches to the text and how the critical engagements with the text have shaped SFF. Engaging with classic works as well as recent books that have been taken up by SFF fans and scholars, the goal of the series is not to be the arbiters of canonical importance, but to show how sustained critical analysis of these texts might bring about a new canon. In addition to their suitability for undergraduate courses, the books will appeal to fans of SFF.

Jerome Winter

BioWare's *Mass Effect*

palgrave
macmillan

Jerome Winter
University of California, Riverside
Riverside, CA, USA

ISSN 2662-8562 ISSN 2662-8570 (electronic)
Palgrave Science Fiction and Fantasy: A New Canon
ISBN 978-3-031-18875-6 ISBN 978-3-031-18876-3 (eBook)
https://doi.org/10.1007/978-3-031-18876-3

This Palgrave Macmillan imprint is published by the registered company Springer Nature Switzerland AG.
The registered company address is: Gewerbestrasse 11, 6330 Cham, Switzerland

CONTENTS

CHAPTER 1

Introduction

The videogame series *Mass Effect*[1] is an exceptional example in popular culture of an original science-fictional franchise of recent vintage that has received both commercial success and critical accolades. Moreover, the videogame pushes the canonical boundaries of how science fiction (SF) as a genre can be experienced and understood in the future. This book provides a sustained analysis of the game developed by the BioWare company and delivers an explanatory framework to limn the landmark reception of *Mass Effect* in videogame history. While offering an original argument about the game, this book also synthesizes the burgeoning body of scholarship on *Mass Effect* for a readership unfamiliar with either the game or the critical conversation on its value. Directed toward readers interested either in videogames or in SF culture more broadly, this book mounts an extended inquiry as to why *Mass Effect* in particular has served as such a representative milestone for such a wide variety of players.

[1] In this book, I wish to focus on *Mass Effect* as a single stand-alone series, not including its later *Andromeda* game or any future sequels in development. The reasons I suggest for this particular focus are manifold but perhaps the most important one is that players regularly conceive *Mass Effect* (2007), *Mass Effect 2* (2010), and *Mass Effect 3* (2012) as three individual chapters in a single coherent narrative. The game designers have acknowledged the longstanding legacy of this practice by their successful release of a remastered edition of the trilogy as one unit simply called *Mass Effect: Legendary Edition* (2021).

© The Author(s), under exclusive license to Springer Nature Switzerland AG 2023
J. Winter, *BioWare's Mass Effect*, Palgrave Science Fiction and Fantasy: A New Canon,
https://doi.org/10.1007/978-3-031-18876-3_1

1

Before the 2021 release of the remastered Legendary edition, the original *Mass Effect* trilogy (2007, 2010, 2012) cemented its place in videogame history as a smash-hit blockbuster franchise that had by 2014 estimates sold over 14 million units. BioWare was initially founded by doctors Ray Muzyka, Greg Zeschuk, and Augustine Yip in 1995 to create a medical diagnostic simulator before expanding into popular role-playing videogames set in licensed universes, such as the Dungeons and Dragons campaign *Baldur's Gate* (1998) and the *Star Wars* product *Knights of the Old Republic* (2011). With *Mass Effect*, BioWare attempted to branch out with an intellectual property that reconfigured an established set of SF videogame staples and conventions. Developed over the course of four years by creative director Casey Hudson, scripted by lead writer Drew Karpyshyn, as well as a large stable of full-time supporting writers, and designed by art director Derek Watts, the first *Mass Effect*'s intricate choice-based storytelling, abundant side missions, and immersive open worlds were celebrated in 2007. The critical consensus concluded that what made this videogame so noteworthy was its enthralling bridging of elaborate narrative-based interactivity and customization with a promising set of ludic gameplay mechanics and the spectacularly rendered surfaces and textures, which constituted a technical leap forward in the three-dimensional modeling and polygonal graphical interface of the time.

With the release of *Mass Effect 2*, the outpouring of critical plaudits accelerated, singling out the videogame for its unique combination of rich storytelling and hypnotic gameplay. The Smithsonian American Art Museum, for instance, included the game in a 2011 historical exhibit as a striking example of the "40-year evolution of video games as an artistic medium". As its prominent position in videogame history solidified, so too emerged the recognition of the *Mass Effect* series as a regrettably overlooked milestone in the SF genre beyond the videogame medium. Hence, in 2012, Gizmodo writer Kyle Munkittrick hailed *Mass Effect* as "the most important science fiction universe of our generation"; this canonizing was echoed, following the release of the 2021 Legendary edition, by Tauriq Moosa in *The Guardian*, who hailed the series as "some of the best sci-fi ever made".

The enthusiastic critical response to *Mass Effect* in the SF community and fandom not only derives from its status as a high-caliber videogame entertainment but from a recognition that it rekindles the well-worn conventions of the SF genre, specifically the familiar subgenre of space opera. Synonymous with the sublime grandeur of its cosmic scale and the vertiginous speeds of its faster-than-light starships, the rambunctious adventure fictions of space opera can be loosely defined by a constellation of narrative memes and storytelling icons, such as alien overlords, galactic empires, psi-powers, future wars, the excavation of ancient artifacts, robot armies, supermassive dreadnaughts, and doomsday devices. For many players, *Mass Effect* brought to fruition the potential of videogames as a medium to reconfigure space opera with a vital freshness. One must hasten to add, however, that such space-opera narratives, in sundry fashion, have tended to gravitate toward videogames as a medium, with many of the most successful and iconic early videogames being attempts to adapt the subgenre to the emerging medium. *Space War!* (1962), originally installed on university mainframes, for instance, is often considered the first videogame, and it embraced the idea of intergalactic conflict in its overblown title. Likewise, the hugely successful *Asteroids* (1979), in which players fend off asteroids and flying saucers in their starfighter, was enjoyed by the masses on coin-operated arcades in bars and pool-halls. The role-playing game *Starflight* (1986), a space exploration game filled with galactic empires, exotic aliens, and androids, became successful for the Sega Genesis home consoles. And the popularity of space-opera videogames hasn't let up, as demonstrated by the popularity of the massively multi-player online role-playing game *Eve Online* (2003), which is still played simultaneously by hundreds of thousands of gamers around the world.

What chiefly distinguishes *Mass Effect* as an innovative contribution to the evolving canon of the SF videogame genre is its heady embrace of these space-opera tropes with an intricate realism of world-building, a depth of characterization, and choice-based, interactive gameplay. Moreover, the immersive long-form storytelling marks a pinnacle of achievement in the SF genre, regardless of medium, given that such dynamics span over a series of three densely written, interlocked, choose-your-own-adventure games. Such dynamic storytelling is additionally supplemented by extra downloadable storylines and the possibility of varying replays of each videogame; all told a single game may take a player on average over a 100 hours to exhaustively complete. True to the pun of its title, then, *Mass Effect* taps into a signal cathartic feature of space opera today. As observed by Roger Luckhurst, space opera "carve[s] out a large chunk of narrative time that acts as a bulwark against the depredations of identity in the late modern world" (23); in other words, the subgenre's extrapolations insulate us from rapid technological change or political and social uncertainty. The widespread appeal of *Mass Effect* to a diverse participatory audience can thus be explained by its canny reworking of the sensationalist appeal of pulp space opera of the 1930s and 1940s. But while *Mass Effect* embraces the over-the-top pulp sensibilities of authors like E.E. "Doc" Smith, Edmond Hamilton, Jack Williamson, or A.E. van Vogt, it also rejects their cardboard characters, black-and-white morality, torturous plotting, and dated ideological baggage.[2] Today's SF critics and audiences often look askance at what is taken to be the naïve, triumphal optimism of pulp-era SF, perhaps best embodied in the swaggering confidence exuded by the space-cop superheroes in Hamilton's Captain Future or the Lensmen in E.E. "Doc" Smith. Unlike the relatively optimistic visions of future progress depicted in these space-opera pulps, the story world of *Mass Effect* consists of a dark, gritty universe that offers little relief from seamy violence, lawless free-market anarchy, authoritarian regimes, and cesspools of extrajudicial vigilante killings. The *Mass Effect* series appeals to a contemporary audience that expects more politically sophisticated world-building and morally ambiguous characterization than pulp space opera. Far from being childish in tone and worldview, the nuanced world-building of *Mass Effect* reflects an increased sensitivity in our own atrocity-laden real world to the devastating legacy of colonial history, the unsettling impact of rapid technological advancement, and the corrosive effects of global capitalism.

Take this case in point as illustration of the self-aware conversation *Mass Effect* conducts with its pulp influences. An optional "loyalty"[3] side mission in *Mass Effect 2* involves investigating an emergency beacon sent from a derelict frigate, the MSV Hugo Gernsback, which crash-landed on a remote tropical planet. The message concerns the presumed-dead father of a Black crewmember, Jacob Taylor, who is under the command of the playable character, Commander Shepard, on the starship SSV Normandy. The rescue mission ends up unraveling a gripping mystery swirling around

[2] This soaring optimism combined with the breathtaking naïveté found in pulp space opera and its speculations about the future led Brian Aldiss to famously call the SF genre as a whole, in a discussion of E.E. "Doc" Smith and A.E. van Vogt, "Wide Screen baroque" (265) and "the billion year spree" (218), later updated to the "trillion year spree", to reflect the gleeful hyperbole heaped on hyperbole characteristic of pulp space opera.

[3] The "loyalty" mechanic in *Mass Effect 2* involves winning over a non-playable squad member by completing an optional side mission, which features a narrative subplot that develops that character. Achieving the loyalty of the squad member makes it probable that the squad character will be more committed to Shepard's leadership and therefore survive the suicide mission to defeat the Collector base at the end of the videogame.

a seamy cargo cult, hallucinatory flora, father-son psychodrama, and corrupt leadership. The mission's savvy homage—in the fact that the frigate is named after the editor largely credited with coining the term "science fiction" and whose pulp magazine *Amazing Stories* serialized what is often considered the first space opera, namely, Edward E. "Doc" Smith's "The Skylark of Space" (1928)—speaks to the medium-is-the-message way the *Mass Effect* videogame series as a whole retrofits antiquated narrative conceits borrowed from pulp-era space-opera conventions. Routinely dismissed then and now by adult readers as mindless escapism, the genre material of classic space opera has nevertheless been reclaimed—and rehabilitated—by generations of science-fiction writers, critics, and fans who have resisted such canon-formation interventions as overly prescriptive. While also bringing dissident changes to the retrograde elements of traditional space opera, *Mass Effect* taps into the resurgent cultural capital of the subgenre, remodeling its kitschy fun for a contemporary audience of digital gamers, while also showcasing how sophisticated space-opera narratives can smuggle in thematic concerns and narrative problematics that are far from unserious or trivial. In particular, *Mass Effect* renders in the space opera form a perplexing moral ambiguity that other big-budget series of the period epitomize for other SF subgenres, such as in the alternate political histories of *BioShock* (2007–2013) and in the cyberpunk-inflected future noir of *Deus Ex* (2000–2013).

The canny revitalization of Gernsbackian space opera in Jacob's loyalty mission, ironically designated "The Gift of Greatness" as its mission title in the game, by no means stands as the sole Easter egg for the hardcore sci-fi buff. The space ronin Samara's loyalty mission in *Mass Effect 2*, for instance, recalls C.L. Moore's "Shambleau", (1933) originally published in the pulp magazine *Weird Tales*. Both space-opera narratives revolve around a Medusa-headed sociopath who lures in unsuspecting victims to meld with their minds in a pseudo-copulatory act of lethal ecstasy. Likewise, the main adversary of the videogame series, the sentient ships called "Reapers", invoke the unnamable, eldritch horrors of H.P. Lovecraft's Cthulhu Mythos, many stories of which were also originally published in *Weird Tales*. While deftly skirting direct copyright infringements, the game series also wears myriad other pulp-era allusions, references, and influences prominently on its genre-savvy sleeves, including, for instance, shout-outs to the body-snatching paranoia of John W. Campbell Jr.'s "Who Goes There?" (1939), first published in Campbell's own *Astounding Science Fiction*, as various characters are violently "indoctrinated" by the Reapers.

Another less blatant throwback would be when space colonies in the outer reaches of the Terminus System are mysteriously slaughtered by shadowy alien hordes, first by the geth in *Mass Effect*, and then by the Collectors in *Mass Effect 2*, which seems to wallow in the xenophobic primal terror of pulp tales of interstellar menace and peril, such as A.E. van Vogt's "Black Destroyer" (1939), also published in *Astounding*.

Indeed, *Mass Effect*'s knowing exhibition of its SF credentials is far too numerous to belabor here. Suffice it to mention that a few of my personal favorites are the thresher maws that closely resemble the sandworms from Frank Herbert's *Dune* (1965), the red-pupiled oculus that visually echoes HAL 9000's panoptic camera eye from Arthur C. Clark and Stanley Kubrick's film *2001: A Space Odyssey* (1968), and the decapitated Statue of Liberty head found in the warehouse of an antiquities smuggler, which immediately calls up the image of an irate Charles Heston screaming in the twist ending of the original film version of *Planet of the Apes* (1968). More diffusely, though, the primary recurring conflict between the variegated organic and synthetic species that forms the narrative cornerstone of the videogame series can trace its literary ancestry back to the robot uprising narratives that permeated pulp-era SF, in both of its polar opposite incarnations of ushering in a wondrous technological utopia—for example, Isaac Asimov's robot series, early stories of which were published in *Astounding*—or leading to technological dystopia and automated enslavement and terror—for example, Jack Williamson's "With Folded Hand" (1947), also published in *Astounding*. For, unlike the bug-eyed monsters that populate other space-operatic videogames such as *Halo* (2001–2020), the original *Mass Effect* series charts the periodic ascendency of a machinic intelligence, the Reapers, that poses an extinction-level threat for all organic life across the fictive galaxy.

Yet the characters in *Mass Effect* also invest in technology through cyborg augmentation and body-modification implants to resist the Reaper invasions. This deep engagement with problematic machines can perhaps best be illustrated by the first mission of the series, on the human space colony Eden Prime. Here the player character Shepard receives eerie visions from a damaged beacon deposited by the extinct alien species called the Protheans, ostensibly wiped out by the Reapers 50,000 years ago. Provided a cipher, this coded message interfaces with the brains of organic individuals and warns of the imminent Reaper invasion, as rendered in a queasy experimental montage of a cut-scene that game designer Casey Hudson created from photographs of circuit boards and screws intermeshed with supermarket meat. The mixture of revelation and terror in this initial narrative gambit testifies to the scrupulous ambivalence over technological progress the videogame sustains over the series. In fact, it is precisely in this complicated stance toward technological progress that *Mass Effect* can be viewed as critically updating pulp-derived genre materials. Likewise, to a more pronounced degree, recent literary space operas by writers such as Iain M. Banks, Alastair Reynolds, Elizabeth Bear, or Becky Chambers, to name only a few vanguard practitioners, provide barbed critiques of the unexamined presumptions, ideological underpinnings, and escapist fantasy of pulp-derived space opera. After all, despite the mind-bending wonder of "Doc" Smith's Lensman saga or Edmond Hamilton's Captain Future series, the clumsy didactic tone, the adolescent-male gadget-fetishism, and the privileging of galaxy-policing, eugenic supermen in these space operas can seem woefully dated to contemporary audiences. Such bygone pulp-era space opera is all the more likely to be remembered by readers today as cringingly backward-looking, that is, continually reenacting a "juvenile fantasy" to use Jacob's ashamed description of his father in "The Gift of Greatness" storyline from *Mass Effect 2*.

Moreover, the cultural politics of space opera today frequently subvert the conciliatory tone of erstwhile space opera. Space opera today frequently rejects the clichéd conventions of pulp fiction as all too easily reinforcing the depredations of global capitalist history, especially the history of technologically dominated colonialism. John Rieder compellingly argues, for instance, that a feature constitutive to the emergence of SF as a genre, and the space-operatic "marvelous voyage" in particular, is "a fantasy of appropriation alluding to real objects and real effects that pervaded and transformed life in the [imperial] homeland" (6). Certainly, such political allegory—what, on a formalistic level, the seminal SF critic Darko Suvin, in *Metamorphoses of Science Fiction*, might term "cognitive estrangement" (7) for the way SF both distorts and mirrors real-world history—is more veiled by genre trappings in the *Mass Effect* series than in literary space-opera proper, as can be expected, given the vast gulf between a narrow, devoted readership and a big-budget, mass-market videogame commodity. Nevertheless, *Mass Effect* can be distinguished from the issues inherent in some other retro-styled, genre-savvy videogames, such as the uncritical recycling of misogynist hard-boiled tropes in Rockstar's *LA Noire* or the rehashing of Native American stereotypes in the neo-western *Red Dead Redemption* (2010). In such a way, *Mass Effect* is more consonant with the critique of Ayn Rand's philosophy in Ken Levine's *BioShock* series. *Mass Effect*'s canny riposte to the nostalgic tendencies of traditional space opera is quite unmistakable.

Indeed, the fundamental premise baked into the *Mass Effect* series explicitly rebukes xenophobia, discrimination, and prejudice. In the future history of the videogame, in the year 2157, humanity excavates a Prothean artifact while surveying Mars, and this relic of a long-dead alien civilization contains a data cache that bootstraps humanity to discover a "mass relay" orbiting Pluto. These mysterious mass relays enable faster-than-light interstellar travel, thus interlinking the galaxy and introducing a future humanity to the hyper-advanced commonwealth of diverse alien species. This galactic federation includes the various species, including the asari, the turians, and the salarians, who have together created a Citadel Council, an elite governing body that loosely rules the explored sectors of the Milky Way. By the in medias res timeline of the first game, following a cease-fire in the First Contact War between the equally militaristic turians and the aggressively colonizing humans, beginning in the year 2183, humanity is being considered for a seat on the Citadel Council. However, humanity is routinely treated with suspicion, aggression, and hostility by alien species at large, who conceive the relative newcomers as disruptive to the status quo of the diverse galactic community.

In *Mass Effect*'s provocative premise, then, humanity has only just arrived on a cosmic scene that stretches back thousands of complicated years. In this space-opera setting, in other words, the enduring myth in the popular imagination of outer space as "the final frontier", to use John F. Kennedy's rhetoric that inaugurated the Cold War's space race, is exploded as a sorely mistaken settler-colonialist fantasy. Rieder calls this final-frontier ideology that transfigures inhabited land into virgin territory the "discoverer's fantasy" (31) in the earlier context of the SF genre's historical emergence. Unlike this fantasy of discovery, though, large portions of the galaxy in *Mass Effect* are already very much pluralistically occupied. Indeed, derogated as an inferior species by adversarial aliens, humanity responds to the naked aggression it meets with across the galaxy by brewing its own xenophobic reactionary politics, embodied by the Terra Firma party. This party is a pro-human, anti-alien radical movement that lobbies for an aggressive colonial expansionism across the outposts of the galaxy on the principle of humanity *über alles*. Regardless of the moral alignment a character player chooses, the underlying script of the videogame series, however, militates against the Terra Firma's standpoint and its xenophobic and even genocidal agenda, given that the overweening threat of Reaper mechanization necessitates the fostering of solidarity among organic species and managing the friction among a disparate galaxy of diverse interests and alien concerns.

The ambivalence toward alien technology that proliferates in the narrative of *Mass Effect* parallels the conflicted relationship of gamers with the technical affordances of the videogame design, especially in the customization of the virtual avatar. Indeed, in the burgeoning scholarship on the videogame, *Mass Effect* neatly straddles both narrative-oriented and gameplay-driven theories for why videogames matter today, intricately bridging long-form storytelling with a variegated set of ludic mechanics. Digital and new-media scholars increasingly adopt a "ludo-narrative" approach to videogame studies, combining critical perspectives that stress both the kinetics of rule-based challenges and skill-driven achievements— pioneered, for instance, in the academic criticism of Espen Aarseth and Jesper Juul—with the interactive criteria of narrative agency, characterology, and meaningful storytelling choice, as explicated, for instance, in the theoretical work of Janet Murray and Marie-Laure Ryan. For instance, in the first *Mass Effect* game, a player creates the look and backstory of their own personal Sheperd. This character can be imported across all three games. A player must choose story-based elements, such as pre-service history, psychological profile, and military specialization, that is, solider, engineer, or infiltrator. These choices have implications for the narrative outcomes and the dynamics of the combat gameplay. The player also can choose between a male or female body type. The player likewise can manipulate their Shepard's facial appearance, skin tone, tattoos, and make-up, to a significant degree, allowing the player to create an avatar that looks like them or to play with a completely different appearance.

As evident in the wide variety of character customization options, exactly who can be considered the author of a *Mass Effect* playthrough remains an unanswerable conundrum. The videogame series pushes the envelope of interactive storytelling, which reaches its limits in what Ian Bogost calls the "procedural" logic inherent in any videogame. Bogost suggests that an iron cage of ideological framing is computationally encoded in the rule-based heuristics and constraint-driven algorithms of the videogame. In other words, regardless of the consumer player's agency and narrative customization, the cultural politics that swirls around the technical production of a videogame reigns supreme: "the machines of industrialization simply act as a particularly tangible medium for expressing these logics" (7). And the procedural rhetoric of *Mass Effect* series does indeed seem to lapse at points into a toxic nostalgia for benevolent technological progress, perhaps best epitomized by the game's load screens that feature gadget-fetishizing blue-print schematics of mass effect relays and weaponized omni-tools.

Nevertheless, far from consisting of automated button-mashing, at its best, the procedural logic of *Mass Effect* affords significant player agency in its ludonarrative design. *Mass Effect* combines both the ludic imperatives of gamified rules, skills, and challenges with the cerebral interplay of genre storytelling and gameplay-driven goals, purposes, and decisions. Some of these gameplay mechanics that will be analyzed in this book include a dialogue wheel that expresses not a selected variety of pre-articulated expressions but rather delicate wisps of thought that are then subsequently verbalized differently by the character. Transgressively, in a signal feature of the videogame that became more inclusive as the series progressed, the player can engage in a same-sex romance and can even romance across the species barrier. The player does so by using the conversational wheel to engage in flirtatious banter, gossip, cheating, expressions of undying ardor, the sharing of deep emotions, sexy chatter, and plans for shore leave. The player also immerses themselves in open-world sandboxes, non-purposively exploring simulated virtual environments in an absorptive experiential flow videogame scholars have referred to as "paideia", listlessly overhearing elevator conversations, shopping for space hamsters, feeding aquarium fish in the captain's quarters, talking with strangers in random street encounters, watching hypersomatic advertisements on kiosks, dancing and drinking at night clubs, or mundanely marking spam email as read.

The diverse gameplay of the videogame both channels and challenges the procedural automations of linear, unified narratives adapted from literary fiction and film, as embodied in its cinematic cut-scenes in which the fanfare of the orchestral score thunders and characters are portrayed through the vocal stylings of bankable Hollywood stars with legendary careers. These virtuosic cut-scenes are paired with other more variable game mechanics such as scavenging and resource management, environment-based puzzle-solving, the memory games of hacking terminals, and mining planets to assist with researching gadget upgrades. The gameplay-infused narrative experience is inextricably intertwined with the overarching speculative dimension of the interstellar future history, especially the diplomatic power plays and the hard-ball political making of enemies and allies that forms its central narrative thread. The stunning aesthetic breakthrough of the *Mass Effect* series derives from its seamless combination of lush three-dimensional animation with the sheer profusion of its immersive narrative and captivating gameplay.

Chapter 2 of this brief primer on the significance of the *Mass Effect* series for a critical understanding of the evolving nature of the SF canon discusses the combination of ludic gameplay and customizable narrative agency in the morality scales of the series. The chapter provides original concrete illustrations for how *Mass Effect* neatly embodies both narrative and interactive theories for why videogames matter today. *Mass Effect* bridges a conventional linear plot cinematic in scope and heavily indebted to the literary subgenre of space opera with both a vastly immersive, non-linear, and open story world and a variegated set of deeply customizable and ludic gameplay mechanics. The chapter therefore explores the morality scale mechanic and its impactful narrative effects, especially as it pertains to the recurring depiction of the choice to prevent or to commit xenocide, or the eradication of a hostile alien species. Given the checkered history of hysterical moral panics to which videogames have often been subjected, the chapter also complicates a reductive idea of identification with a simulated character's moral choices for the more nuanced concept of an estranged affinity with a character's speculative world.

Chapter 3 explores the narrative treatment of globalized realpolitik and social justice, and the way the game cleaves open opportunities for players to undercut the Machiavellian diplomacy and neoliberal nostalgia endemic to the combat scenarios of third-person shooters, and their endless rehearsals of neo-imperialist victimhood narratives and grievance politics of political underdogs facing down insurmountable odds. Complex moral calculus, technology-induced vertigo, and baroque political diplomacy are signal staples of much contemporary space-opera literature; the densely scripted, team-generated writing in *Mass Effect* popularizes these literary space-opera conventions for a mass audience. *Mass Effect* redoubles the intricate realpolitik underpinnings of the science-fictional universe through the novel form of an intensely dialogue-heavy role-playing game sensitive to diverse character customization, regardless as to whether a player chooses to become more of a renegade or more of a paragon. As such, the series allegorizes the struggle of culture-driven coalition-building, strategic diplomatic maneuvering, and strenuous democratic governance as forces that can reverse naked xenophobic aggression, economic disparity, and the insidious legacy of imperialism. This chapter discusses specific case studies from the videogame in which becoming a reluctant celebrity spokesman for a humbled and insecure humanity forces players to negotiate forming tenuous multilateral relationships with a teeming menagerie of suspicious and dismissive alien species; in such a way, the exploding confetti of competing political narratives in *Mass Effect* undermines monolithic ideologies that enforce the status quo.

Chapter 4 involves the narrative gameplay of romancing a paramour in the videogame series and the evident appeal of these chosen story arcs for queer, nonwhite, and feminist fandoms to resist the racism, sexism, and homophobia that pervades the videogame medium. The range of sexualities and genders available for the player character, the development of complex queer characters and people of color throughout the narrative, and the dynamics of cross-species alien romance ensured that *Mass Effect* would become a pivotal touchstone for queer, Black, and feminist fandoms and subcultures. While puritanical watchdogs decried its scandalous cut-scene depictions of sex and reactionary #Gamergate backlash appropriated videogame identity representation as a site of dubious contestation, for vibrant communities self-identified as LGBTQ, people of color, and feminists, *Mass Effect* overcame some of the predominant and retrograde heteronormative, masculinist, and racist trappings of popular science-fictional and videogame culture. This chapter includes a brief discussion of the award-winning literary space-opera writers Catherynne M. Valente and N.K. Jemisin's tie-in novels to the *Mass Effect* universe and their contributions to making the transmedia blitz, alongside videogames, animated movies, and various merchandise, less oriented toward white heterosexual men. This chapter includes a synthesis of which elements in the collaborative storytelling of *Mass Effect* have inspired players, designers, bloggers, critics, scholars, and activists to view the videogame as an ally in the ongoing project to resist mainstream hierarchies and exclusions and to forge a more inclusive and diverse future for SF and general culture.

Chapter 5 then enters into the ongoing debate over the educational value of commercial videogames and examines the way the series engages with significant issues related to science and technology. *Mass Effect* has been hailed by working scientists for its incorporation of data of interest to the ongoing astronomical hunt for extrasolar planets (exoplanets, for short) and for its more or less plausible astrobiological speculations on profoundly different alien physiology. The surprising pedagogical efficacy of this commercial videogame revives the Gernsbackian credo of science education characteristic of pulp space opera. Many professional scientists testify that the attitude toward science in SF texts was formative in their intellectual upbringing. This chapter discusses how the immersive gameplay of *Mass Effect* updates the usefulness of SF as a tool for capturing the popular imagination into a more critical and probing engagement with scientific knowledge. More than traditional science communication and outreach, the game dynamics of *Mass Effect* promises to reach a mass audience. This widened reach is exploited by the games not only to reject a blanket post-truth distrust of science but to productively interrogate the political, cultural, and ethical underpinnings of scientific authority. It is therefore significant that its treatment of astronomy is deeply rooted in current scientific data and theoretical research, such as theories of "hot jupiters" and "super Earths" that have recently transformed our understanding of the formation of solar systems, planets, and the search for alien life. Likewise, the chapter discusses how the radical cognitive weirdness of the alien look and feel in the game derives from plausible speculations on evolutionary theories of competition and cooperation drawn from biology, such as the tough carapace of the crocodilian turians, the eidetic memory of the reptilian drell, and parthenogenesis as a reproductive strategy for the cephalopod-adjacent asari.

Perhaps the proper way to end an introductory chapter for a critical book on *Mass Effect* is to invoke a utopian phrase that recurs with interesting variations over the series. The phrase is from the invented language "Khelish", used by an enviro-suited alien species known as the quarians. The quarians are a diasporic community exiled to a migrant flotilla of generation starships following the misbegotten creation of a vengeful artificial intelligence called the geth who exiled them from their home planet Rannoch. In English, the untranslatable phrase roughly means "by the home world I hope to see one day" and constitutes an all-purpose epithet of profound hope, anger, shock, love, and pride. The phrase is also a final farewell issued by an evolved geth before he sacrifices himself to save the galaxy from the Reaper invasion. In general, the phrase, though, is customary for send-offs prior to embarking on a nomadic journey that will eventually lead to a return home. It therefore seems entirely appropriate to extend the same well-wishing to the intrepid reader of this expeditionary trip into the relatively uncharted zone of our new SF canon. *Keelah Se'lai*.[4]

REFERENCES

Aldiss, Brian. 1974. *The Billion Year Spree: The True History of Science Fiction*. New York: Schocken Books.
BioWare. 2007. *Mass Effect 1*. BioWare. PC/Mac/Consoles.
———. 2010. *Mass Effect 2*. BioWare. PC/Mac/Consoles.
———. 2012. *Mass Effect 3*. BioWare. PC/Mac/Consoles.
———. 2021. *Mass Effect: Legendary Edition*. BioWare. PC/Mac/Consoles.
Bogost, Ian. 2007. *Persuasive Games: The Expressive Power of Videogames*. Cambridge: MIT Press.
Luckhurst, Roger. 2005. *Science Fiction*. Cambridge: Polity.
Mousa, Touriq. 2021. Why Mass Effect Is Some of the Best Sci-Fi Ever Made. *The Guardian*, August 14. https://www.theguardian.com/games/2021/aug/14/why-mass-effect-is-some-of-the-best-sci-fi-ever-made
Munkittrick, Kyle. 2012. Why *Mass Effect* is the Most Important Science-Fiction Universe of Our Generation. *Io9*, February 7. https://gizmodo.com/why-mass-effect-is-the-most-important-science-fiction-u-5886178.
Rieder, John. 2008. *Colonialism and the Emergence of Science Fiction*. Middletown: Wesleyan University Press.
Suvin, Darko. 1979. *Metamorphoses of Science Fiction: On the Poetics and History of a Literary Genre*. New Haven: Yale University Press.

[4]As a testament to the game's popularity, this phrase has entered the general lexicon outside its usage in the narrative to *Mass Effect*. Indeed, in a tongue-in-cheek fashion, the phrase was programmed into Amazon's virtual assistant Alexa. A person can ask Alexa this command query: "does this unit has a soul?" When a geth, Legion, asks the same question before sacrificing himself to save the galaxy from the Reapers, a quarian squad member, Tali'Zorah, replies, "the answer to your question was yes". The geth then replies: "Keelah Se'lai". Alexa replies with the same phrase followed by a "my friend", implying perhaps a brokered peace between people and their assistant Frankenstein's monsters.

CHAPTER 2

"I Don't Know What to Do with Grey": Ludic Gameplay and Narrative Agency

The various character customizations of the player avatar in the *Mass Effect* series, with both their ludic and narrative effects, transform the dimensions of the restyled space-opera genre conventions. One of the defining characteristics of more recent space opera, after all, is its pitting of questionable protagonists, unsympathetic characters, and rebarbative moral ambiguities against the uncritical depiction of diabolic villainy and saintly heroism in classic space opera that was, to be fair, more boundary-pushing, in other ways, in its own time. Other contemporary videogames such as the *Fall Out* series provide character customization options that feature amoral personality traits unattached to morality scales. Philosophically, these videogame affordances may be equally interpreted as either pluralistic or nihilistic in their moral orientation. In contrast, *Mass Effect* includes a psychological profile as part of the initial character customization. For instance, if a player chooses "war hero", they are given a backstory involving Shepard fending off a relentless military assault and earning a rare medal for heroism called the Star of Terra, thus granting the player in the videogame metrics a "paragon" bonus point, a reputation metric that influences how non-player characters (NPCs) interact with and respond to the player in the game.

Mass Effect also builds amoral calibration into the complicated quandaries of its core narrative and gameplay. For instance, if a character chooses as their pre-service history to be "a spacer", that is, to having a

J. Winter, *BioWare's Mass Effect*, Palgrave Science Fiction and Fantasy: A New Canon, https://doi.org/10.1007/978-3-031-18876-3_2

military-brat childhood shaped by parents who worked for the Alliance military, shuffling their avatar's early life aboard starships and space stations. Presumably, in the narrative logic of the game such spacer players have also become terrestrially unmoored due to their early life experience, a trait that is cherished in the space-marine milieu of the game; hence, if one chooses the "spacer" pre-service history, the superior officer, Captain Anderson, raves that "military service runs in the family", in voice-over, while a cinematic frame zooms out from the glowing curvature of the Earth to reveal Shepard staring out a spaceship's observation window.

In the story world, Anderson's impressed comment explains why Shepard is plucked up from relative obscurity for the pivotal Eden Prime mission by the higher-up military brass. Indeed, such a comment, heightened by these sublime Olympian visuals and a pulsing industrial score, also clearly draws on the established space-operatic tradition of "spacers" having extricated themselves from provincial concerns and the ideological prejudices of the Earthborn. Such usage of the term "spacer" has been widespread in SF fiction and fandom for generations, recurring often in works like Isaac Asimov's influential *Foundation* series (1942–1986) and Samuel R. Delany's beloved short story "Aye, and Gomorrah" (1967). In the abstract terms of genre criticism, the radical estrangement and alterity of the spacer's decentered viewpoint is in a dialectic with the rationalized reality of the audience's own historical, empirical world. As Carl Freedman writes, the SF genre inevitably concerns a future history that is "not only one different in time or place from our own, but one whose chief interest is precisely the difference that such difference makes" (43).

Alternatively, if a player chooses "ruthless" as their psychological profile, the game bestows upon the player a "renegade" reputation point. The ruthless character does not let moral quandaries interfere with his or her dedication to the mission regardless of the human cost. This profile can be combined with the pre-service history of being "Earthborn", which consists of a character growing up in the criminal underworld of one of Earth's dystopian cities. In the opening voice-over for this character customization, Anderson's comments suggest a more grudging admiration about Shepard having been "raised on the streets" and having to "look out" only for number one. The narrative implication here seems to be that the grisly expedience of such an upbringing has instilled in this Shepard's pre-service history a pragmatic willingness to rationalize complicity with violence and corruption for the sake of survival and self-preservation. However, the ultimate representation of this moral ambiguity is the "sole survivor" pre-service history in which a traumatized Shepard miraculously defies near-certain death in a thresher maw attack; the videogame awards this Shepard, morally bruised but not beaten, both a bonus paragon and renegade point. In this sole survivor option, Anderson defends his choice with a more complicated assessment: "every soldier has scars".

Overall, the moral bearings of the character are subordinated by the game design to the epic world-building of the future history, such that, as Istvan Csicsery-Ronay, Jr. claims about the SF genre more categorically, the individual character choices are subsumed by "megahistories of the human species as a single great collective actor, and the personal histories of protagonists in a critical moment of that covering megahistory" (82). The morality scale extends beyond contingent subjective choices to the collaborative storytelling of the sociological worldview and narrative structure of the videogame, especially given the character is initially cus-tomized. Once the story-based gameplay begins, the player starts deciding between a rapid succession of paragon and renegade options on dialogue wheels and interruption opportunities during the cinematic cut-scenes. In the first two *Mass Effect* games, the morality metric measures one's repu-tational progress on separate scales, as opposed to a single scale in which quantifiable moral actions are in sum balanced toward either the light or dark sides, as featured in BioWare's earlier Star Wars game *The Knights of the Old Republic*. The coexistence of renegade and paragon benchmark bars underscores the complexity of the game's morality scale, even if hav-ing certain thresholds of renegade or paragon scores separately unlock further renegade and paragon options once the narrative unfolds. In a ludonarrative affordance, the renegade and paragon choices are also cou-pled to experience points, which can help upgrade one's combat skill lev-els, and which therefore directly impacts the most intensely ludic aspects of the third-person-shooter gameplay, as discussed in more depth in Chap. 3.

The fact that renegade alternatives, some of which are quite repugnant, exist at all in the story world bestows meaningful agency on the player avatar's choices. Nevertheless, despite all the labor that goes into crafting these renegade options, BioWare's reported in-house data reveals a near totality of players prefer the morally enlightened options.[1] This fact resists the stereotyping of gamers as morally depraved and dangerous misfits popular in mass media. Still, an important distinction about the narrative power of renegade actions needs to be highlighted here, one through which the fictional storytelling of *Mass Effect* transcends the overly moralistic tone of earlier space opera. Even when the player identifies with a renegade choice, this gameplay option does not automatically equate to a player endorsing, at its most extreme, a bigoted, sadistic, or pathological dialogue option or plot event. Despite the aspirational optimism of the space-opera setting, the disquieting limits of moral agency in the videogame series instead frequently elicit a troubled, contestatory effect that one of the game's principal antiheroic characters, Garrus Vakarian, expresses to Shepard in one of a number of guilt-stricken tête-à-têtes in *Mass Effect 2*: "So much easier seeing the world in black and white. Grey? I don't know what to do with grey." Consider the murky aspects, for instance, of this minor but entirely typical example of the morality gameplay dynamic. During a brief side quest in *Mass Effect 2*, Shepard may choose to take the edge off and order a drink at the bar, in the Afterlife nightclub on the anarchic, libertarian outpost of Omega. After recovering from a poisoned drink served up by the bartender Forvan, a member of an anti-human four-eyed alien species called batarians, Shepard can strike up another conversation with Forvan and choose the red-tinted renegade option on the dialogue wheel. This option leads to Shepard ordering another drink from the batarian and forcing Forvan through verbal threats to drink the newly poisoned drink. The intimidated alien duly swallows his comeuppance and promptly collapses.

On a purely moralistic level, it is difficult to sympathize with Shepard's revenge game here, even if a player writes such behavior off as the cruel antics of a noirish, disaffected antihero. In contrast, the blue-tinted paragon dialogue-wheel option simply has Shepard loudly complain to a surly turian patron that Forvan is notoriously prone to speciesism and has been caught red-handed poisoning his non-batarian customers, thus instigating the incensed turian into shooting the homicidal bartender. While less directly culpable, this odd technicality of aiding and abetting the murder of

---

[1] In a February 2020 tweet, BioWare's cinematic designer John Ebenger revealed the in-house data that "something like 92%" of players chose paragon options in response to a joke of the player who was surprised at how much they chose the paragon options in a space opera that seems to endorse breaking taboos.

the bartender in revenge, instead of coercing a poisoner into suicide, will still likely strike many players as almost equally morally loathsome, perhaps satirically so. Without pretending to authorize such brutal violence, an important way to reconcile either the paragon or renegade behavior with the narrative is by way of understanding the world-building megahistory of *Mass Effect*, which the player can look up in the game through a text-based archive called the Codex that one collects while exploring the mission environments and the open-world sandboxes of the videogame. Reading the Codex will inform the player, for instance, that batarians—considered a dangerous rogue species by the Council—harbor an aggressive grudge against humanity for their expansionist attempt to colonize the batarian territories on the Skyllian Ridge region of the galaxy in the early 2160s.

As the above example illustrates, far from subscribing to a straightforward moral calculus between exhibiting a black hat or white hat to NPCs, the morality scale does not reinforce reductive binaries between altruism and self-interest, or to be less charitable, between coming off as either more of a prig or more of a cretin. To the frustration of players who crave the moral neatness of relatable heroes and unlikable heavies in their genre entertainments, and to the delight of players who upbraid censorship in their escapist fun, player decisions in *Mass Effect* frequently do not impact narrative outcomes as much as one might expect. However, the inconsequential nature of the morality scale is a fascinating science-fictional feature and not a bug of the videogame series. Arguing for a more nuanced analysis of how audiences respond to a fictional constructed world of a story, instead of a straightforward identification with characters, Rita Felski provides a useful critical toolkit that is resonant here with how the morality scales in *Mass Effect* help players emotionally invest in their avatars.[2]

[2] Felski is responding critically to John Frow's seminal work *Character and Person*; interestingly, in that theoretical book, which essentially delineates the notion of a character as based on ideas of personhood that are themselves deeply fictional and imaginary, Frow uses digital games to illustrate the distinction between the "moral effect" of liking or not liking from the psychological experience of fantasizing and projecting (41–9). For a brief history of widespread academic and popular uses of the term "identification" to describe the way a player assumes the traits of an avatar character in a videogame, as opposed to the process of "projection" in which an avatar character reflects the traits of a player, see Luca Papale's "Beyond Identification: Defining the Relationships Between Player and Avatar". Papale proposes complicating the oversimplistic notion of "identification" with the ideas of empathy, sympathy, and detachment as well, concepts that have overlap with Felski's terms discussed in this chapter.

While not discussing specifically the intellectual puzzle of how different versions of the same essential videogame character can differ so greatly, Felski interrogates the ever-changing aspects of characters in the related context of fan fiction, which "testifies to the highly translatable aspects of characters, their potential to be reborn in new contexts" (86). Emphasizing that creating ironic distance from fictional characters can be just as effective a fictional technique as identification with characters, Felski suggests that felt affinity with world-building, as opposed to mere characterization, can be taxonomized as "alignment" (the extent of narrative time the world a character inhabits receives), "allegiance" (an evaluation of how an audience affiliates with certain political and ethical values espoused by a character's world), "recognition" (an affective response of seeing one's own traits mirrored in a character's world), and "empathy" (feeling with and for a character's world). These engrossing forms of narrative identification oriented toward character-driven worlds make the morality scales in *Mass Effect* less a perfunctory encounter with the design parameters of a computer program and more of an innovative experience with the arresting power of space opera.

When comparing the irresolvable double binds that arise in paragon and renegade playthroughs, narrative alignment with and ethical allegiance to a player's own particular Shepard can decisively clash. For instance, in the first *Mass Effect*, Shepard recruits Urdnot Wrex, a fierce warrior of the krogan species. The krogans are a bellicose race of hump-backed saurian bruisers from the post-apocalyptic planet Tuchanka, who were once poised to be fruitful and multiply, savagely conquering the galaxy in the process. This galactic expansionism occurred before the salarians manufactured a sterilizing virus, the "genophage", at the behest of the turians who demanded the stop of the unchecked spread. Shepard completes an obligatory mission with Wrex and can go on an optional mission to help Wrex retrieve his family's armor. During missions and on the Normandy, Shepard has many opportunities to engage in conversation with Wrex and become emotionally enmeshed with the affable but barbaric krogan's gruff attitude and wry outlook on life. By the time a player has reached the eerily lovely planet of Virmire, where Saren Arterius, the rogue black-ops turian who is the main adversary of the first game, has occupied a laboratory with the aim of breeding an army of alien mercenaries, Shepard has already had ample opportunity to get attached to Wrex.

Yet because Saren's scientists have cured the genophage in order to breed a krogan army, a complicated moral-ethical event horizon arises. A player's unique political and social allegiances, personal norms, and ideological value systems now literally come into play. Given the historical trauma the genophage has wreaked on his people who are now living through an extinction vortex, Wrex is adamantly opposed to the salarian Captain Kirrahe's plan to destroy the genophage in the siege of the enemy base. The salarian, of course, has the ulterior motive of seeking to prevent another reign of krogan terror across the galaxy. After hearing from the salarian, a player may notice Wrex firing off random rounds of his shotgun in indignant rage on the beach behind the infiltration regiment's camp.

Approaching the unhinged Wrex on Virmire's beach engages a player's values since destroying the genophage cure is essentially perpetuating a war crime, namely, inflicting a sterilizing disease on enemy combatants. At this point in the game the player has most likely gained enough morality points, translated to intimidation and charm points in the first game, to unlock alternative narrative branches that may align with the player's real-life morality. The player's antipathy to the genophage might guide them to choose the charm-unlocked dialogue option that will successfully save Wrex's life by convincing him that assisting Saren, who has been indoctrinated by the Reapers, will only end up being even more catastrophic for the already beleaguered krogan species. If the player chooses the charm option and Wrex survives here, the player will cheerfully meet up with the krogan multiple times throughout the entire series; if Wrex dies, those future encounters are foreclosed, and for the rest of the first game a memorial shadow of Wrex haunts the screen where mission squad mates are selected. The narrative drive of *Mass Effect*, as opposed to a player's own moral allegiances, forces a player to continue pursuing the overriding goal of defeating Saren and the Reapers at all costs. If players do not have enough charm or intimidation points to save Wrex, they choose from the less desirable paragon and renegade options available to them. If one renegade action is selected, Shepard signals the xenophobic human Ashley Williams to shoot Wrex with a sniper rifle. Players are forced to ruminate over the morality of the character choices before committing to a course of action, but they will also likely bristle with disappointment over all the available outcomes. The ironic distance the game opens up between a player and a character disturbs easy identification.

In these moral conundrums, *Mass Effect* stresses not only the traditional notion of honorable military sacrifice but, more probingly, an inevitable complicity with xenophobic regimes. If a player chooses the inferior paragon option in the Vimire mission, the intolerant Ashley still murders

Wrex at least partly because of her own reactionary dogmatic hostility toward aliens, which stems from her personal family shame of having a grandfather who surrendered to the turians at Shanxi during the First Contact War. These personal dilemmas are inextricably steeped in the fantastic colonial and material megahistories of a densely imagined future galaxy. In this way, and much akin to the ambivalent portrayals of the issue in sophisticated literary space opera today, a complex irony governs the interplay of empathy and sympathy in *Mass Effect*'s complex, recurring treatment of alien genocide, that is, xenocide. The convergence of capitalism-driven technological progress and the genocidal wiping out of foreign cultures has, after all, preoccupied space opera since its pulp inception, as outlined by Darko Suvin who traces the passing of the "genocide torch" ("Of Starship Troopers and Refuseniks", 123) from pulp-era space-opera scribes Jack Williamson and Edmond Hamilton to Robert Heinlein's nuanced yet jingoistic treatment of the controversial theme in the polarizing novel *Starship Troopers* (1959).

Despite Heinlein's opposition to totalitarian rhetoric, the intelligent Arachnid alien species in *Starship Troopers* are slandered as repellently hive-minded "bugs" and, after Buenos Aires is genocidally annihilated by the aliens, the juvenile space-marine hero, Juan Rico, leads a platoon to capture the Arachnid queen at the novel's climax. With a decisively more critical bent, *Mass Effect* updates this Cold War space-opera trope in its depiction of Shepard's encounter with the insectoid Rachni species. Under the covert funding of Saren and the equally Reaper-indoctrinated asari Matriarch Benezia, the questionable Binary Helix corporation has been conducting illegal experiments on the last remaining Rachni Queen in their scientific hot labs on the ice planet Noveria. Binary Helix attempts to experiment on the Rachni Queen's brood warriors in the interest of creating an unstoppable army, but her children go feral without her guiding presence. After defeating Benezia in combat, Shepard confronts one of the most pivotal moral conundrums of the series. Shepard must choose between the paragon option of showing empathy for the Rachni Queen and the renegade option of siding with the Council of alien species. If Shepard chooses the renegade option, this potential galactic threat of the Rachni will be eliminated; if Shepard chooses the paragon option, the historical wrong of xenocide will be righted.

As documented by historians of genocide in the copious literature on the subject, the portrayal of the scapegoated victims of legitimated state violence as monstrous insects that need to be ethnically cleansed is conventional in totalitarian propaganda. In dehumanizing a foreign species through the trope of the aggressive alien bug, Heinlein's *Starship Troopers*, along with an endless host of other largely forgotten space operas through the years, falls prey to this popular rhetoric. The SF novelist John Kessel, in the essay "Creating the Innocent Killer", highlights a curious logic of such work with regards to Orson Scott Card's space opera about the xenocide of insectoid "buggers", *Ender's Game* (1985). Kessel argues that by scapegoating the victims as the victimizers, or the to-be-exterminated as potential exterminators, "those of us concerned about understanding the 'other' are redirected from worrying about the alien, and thus our condemnation of genocide re-emerges as a sign of our prejudice and small-mindedness".

Such a standard justification of genocide as a reasonable response to a possible attack indeed accompanies the player's moral deliberation in *Mass Effect*. Shepard must choose between annihilating the captured Rachni Queen in an acid tank, the renegade option, and releasing her to roam free in outer space, the paragon option. The Codex explains that the Rachni Wars, which occurred approximately two millennia prior to the game's timeline, flared up when the Rachni, roused from a peaceful isolationism, hijacked the faster-than-light technology of an expeditionary force, proceeding to outnumber and devastate the military forces of the Council. The galactic menace of aggressive intelligent insects spread unabated until the salarians uplifted the krogans to invade the Rachni's home world of Suen and seemingly eradicate the species by detonating bombs in their Queen's underground nests. Given this intricate future history, it makes sense that Shepard is later remonstrated by the turian councilor if the player decides to release the Rachni Queen. The councilor barks, "I hope you're right, Shepard. Our children's children will pay the price if you're not." Perhaps in an implicit acknowledgment of this possibility, and the idea that, as Felski puts it, "empathy is soaked through with power and privilege" (106) in its sentimental outpouring for the victims whose unjust oppression one otherwise complicitly enables, *Mass Effect* does not allow its players to sit comfortably with an act of benevolence, that is, the ostensibly humane choice of sparing a hostile species its self-sown extinction.

The paragon option of releasing the Rachni Queen, and thereby showing empathy for the otherized alien, receives a significant amount of positive reinforcement during later narrative developments in *Mass Effect*. From a postcolonial viewpoint, Joan Gordon suggests that the xenocidal trope that pervades space opera turns on a genre fulcrum of SF cognitive estrangement: either the estrangement of "colonizers [who] attempt to absorb an alien culture by familiarizing it" or "in the attempt to erase an alien culture in the act of genocide, the alien-contact novel insists upon 'cognition', recognition of the violence and injustice of the act" (209). The game enlists such a postcolonial recognition of systemic injustice in the service of an eerie scene in which Shepard converses with the Rachni Queen. Possessing the shambling dead body of an asari commando, the Rachni Queen speaks in a whispery echo through garbled, poetic expressions that demonstrate that the sentient, hive-minded species can perceive the synesthetic "songs" and "colors" of the cosmos that are all but incommunicable to planetary humanoids who live in the "low spaces". The cognitively estranged alterity of this alien-contact narrative also flatly contradicts the renegade justification for xenocide given that the Rachni Queen testifies it no longer experiences the "sour yellow note" that contributed to its historical bout of expansionist rampage. Indeed, the second and third *Mass Effect* games corroborate the Rachni Queen's testimony given that if one chooses a paragon option the Rachni Queen later warns Shepard of an incoming invasion prior to a devastating Reaper attack on Earth and then pitches in to support as a war asset in the building of an armada to finally defeat the Reapers. If one chooses the renegade option, history repeats itself as brutal farce, and, in *Mass Effect 3*, Shepard must again destroy a mutant Rachni brood surrogate that the Reapers have created.

In addition to the interplay of empathy and sympathy, characterization in *Mass Effect* also depends upon a dramatic register of recognition to cement the virtual affinity a gamer develops with their player avatar. Felski defines recognition as both the raw power and the deep insight that happens when connecting with a character as a familiar but different version of one's own selfhood. Felski illustrates the concept through the responses generations of readers have had to the existential antihero, Meursault, in Albert Camus's *The Stranger* (1942) and "the common inability to feel the appropriate, socially sanctioned emotions" (115). Far from the virtue-signaling hero worship of traditional space opera, character development in *Mass Effect* might provoke such shocks of recognition in players precisely because the characters may strike players as tapping into the reality of their own personal experience, radiating out such existentially antisocial and disgruntled temperaments that speak to the player's own private reserves of cynicism, irony, and darkness. Such a recognition of affinity with disaffected characters overlays the SF world-building and its powerful representations of the anxieties and fantasies endemic to our technologically saturated modern life. This genre effect explains why the experience of playing *Mass Effect* can seem so staggering and immersive to gameplayers, especially perhaps to players who may not be well-acquainted with this habitual pairing of deep characterization and complex realism that pervades contemporary SF literature.

Take, for instance, the female character introduced in *Mass Effect 2* who assumes the fairy-tale moniker of Jack. This roguish misfit has cultivated notoriety as a galactically wanted outlaw, a brigand who cuts an impressive figure as a bald, tattooed, foul-mouthed mash-up of a futuristic Belle Starr and a cyborg Sinead O'Connor. Jack has been imprisoned in a mercenary prison-ship *Purgatory* for a crime spree that includes murder, brigandry, and kidnapping. At this point in the narrative saga, Shepard has made a Faustian compact with the private military contractors, Cerberus, to fend off the immediate threat of the Reapers. Cerberus is a fringe human-supremacist faction reviled by the Council for its unethical eugenic experimentation, terrorism, sabotage, and assassinations. It is led by the Illusive Man, who only communicates with Shepard through the remote telepresence of a hologram. After Shepard rescues Jack from this hyper-automated, corrupt private prison-ship *Purgatory*, the player slowly learns Jack's backstory. As a child, she was Subject Zero, a non-consensual participant in Cerberus's experiments at the Teltin facility on the mutant planet Pragia. Due to Jack's accidental exposure in the womb to "Element Zero", a fictional substance discovered in *Mass Effect*'s future history that causes electromagnetic superpowers called "biotics", Cerberus physically and psychologically tortures, and repeatedly nearly murders, the orphan child Jack under the xenophobic banner of protecting humankind from alien threats. Cerberus hones her biotic powers to such an overwhelming extent that she escapes the research facility during an inmate riot, thus commencing her post-adolescent brigandry across the galaxy.

Jack understandably nurses a vengeful grudge against Cerberus for their formative brutal experimentation on her body and mind, even though the Illusive Man unconvincingly disavows culpability when confronted by Shepard, claiming the research facility had gone rogue. Jack is belligerent in her interactions with Shepard, only tentatively agreeing to join the Normandy crew once Shepard oversteps their authority and discloses Jack's classified Cerberus files to the new crewmember. Once she receives these files, Jack warms up to Shepard, and, in the neon red-drenched lower engineering decks of the ship, a player can choose to engage in twisted flirtatious banter about abandoning the galaxy-saving mission, turning pirate, and executing civilians. During one such exchange, Jack hatefully berates Shepard as a "Cerberus lapdog" and "military stooge" before flatly confessing to "murder, assault, kidnapping, drugs, stealing, and arson". The player can earn renegade points by sympathizing with these lonely, dark confessions. In her loyalty mission in *Mass Effect 2*, Jack enlists Shepard's help in exploding a bomb that destroys the abandoned Teltin facility as a way to cathartically rid herself of her vengeful obsession.

On this loyalty mission, Shepard accompanies a traumatized Jack on a tour of the facility, including a gladiatorial arena in which the experimenters used implants, drugs, and operant conditioning techniques to reward lethal savagery in combat. Found holographic recordings during gameplay reveal that Cerberus used other patients as to perfect their studies on Jack, thus giving Jack more survivor's guilt and also diminishing her edgy confidence that only her exceptional individualism has ensured her survival. In one of the game's most disturbing renegade choices, Shepard can coach the mentally unstable Jack to shoot in cold blood a deranged ex-patient, ostensibly to liberate Jack from her own trauma. The availability of such a lurid, malevolent choice might seem to reinforce the checkered history of moral panics videogames and table-top role-playing fantasy have recurrently engendered in the public sphere.[3] Arguably, though, *Mass Effect* exhibits an uncompromising moral imagination in scripting such cathartically extreme revenge fantasies, which speak to players who may recognize unflattering aspects of their own maladjusted personalities in such sociopathic behavior. Jack herself expresses this therapeutic embrace of caustic self-pity when she movingly tells Shepard: "that victim garbage, it's half me". Of course, in a less demented playthrough, a player can also earn paragon points for talking Jack back from the ledge during the "Subject Zero" mission at the Teltin facility, thus sparing the pitiable life of the other traumatized ex-patient, Jack's dark double. If the player chooses to play the Teltin mission at all, the newly galvanized Jack will survive the suicide mission at the end of *Mass Effect 2*. There is even an option to romance Jack, either in a meaningless fling or in a long-lasting emotional relationship, but only if one's Shepard is male since Jack is scripted as

---

[3] For a book-length study on how such moral panics inform negative stereotyping of gamers in SF literary fiction, see Barr (2018). For a larger critical overview that tackles the long history of moral panics and videogames, see Markey and Ferguson (2017).

straight, despite being originally programmed as pansexual. Jack's powerful plot arc then continues into *Mass Effect* 3 where a semi-redeemed Jack has morphed into a vitriolic but highly respected and even deeply caring teacher of biotically enhanced children at the much more ethical Alliance-operated Grissom Academy.

In sum, the morality scales of *Mass Effect* cannot be said to represent either a didactic altruism or a cynical nihilism. The morality scales instead actively meld real players with their virtual avatars into a feedback loop of variable emotional investment. This affinity is established through the combination of ludic gameplay and narrative elements that promotes profound interest in, if not exactly identification with, characters. This highly iterative characterization updates and reconfigures the staid moralism of traditional literary space opera, significantly enhancing the videogame's engagement with the disturbing conundrums of contemporary history as well, especially in the recurring SF portrayals of eugenics, xenocide, and the depredations of techno-capitalist progress. Scholars have long studied how such a profound cognitive effect is precisely what makes masterworks of the SF genre so culturally transformative.

References

Barr, Jason. 2018. *Video Gaming in Science Fiction: A Critical Study*. Jefferson: McFarland.

BioWare. 2007. *Mass Effect 1*. BioWare. PC/Mac/Consoles.

———. 2010. *Mass Effect 2*. BioWare. PC/Mac/Consoles.

———. 2012. *Mass Effect 3*. BioWare. PC/Mac/Consoles.

———. 2021. *Mass Effect: Legendary Edition*. BioWare. PC/Mac/Consoles.

Csicsery-Ronay, Istvan. 2008. *The Seven Beauties of Science Fiction*. Middletown: Wesleyan University Press.

Felski, Rita. 2019. Identifying with Characters. In *Character: Three Inquiries in Literary Studies*, ed. Amanda Anderson, Rita Felski, and Toril Moi, 77–126. Chicago: Chicago University Press.

Freedman, Carl. 2000. *Critical Theory and Science Fiction*. Middletown: Wesleyan University Press.

Frow, John. 2014. *Character and Person*. Oxford: Oxford University Press.

Gordon, Joan. 2002. Utopia, Genocide, and the Other. In *Edging into the Future: Science Fiction and Contemporary Cultural Transformation*, ed. Veronica Hollinger and Joan Gordon, 205–216. Philadelphia: University of Pennsylvania Press.

Kessel, John. 2004. Creating the Innocent Killer: *Ender's Game,* Intentions, and Morality. *Foundation, the International Review of Science Fiction* 33 (90). http://johnjosephkessel.wixsite.com/kessel-website/creating-the-innocent-killer

Markey, Patrick, and Christopher Ferguson. 2017. *Moral Combat: Why the War on Violent Video Games is Wrong.* Dallas: BenBella Books.

Papale, Luca. 2014. Beyond Identification: Defining the Relationships Between Player and Avatar. *Journal of Game Criticism* 1 (2), http://gamescriticism.org/articles/papale-1-2

Suvin, Darko. 2008. Of Starship Troopers and Refuseniks: War and Militarism in U.S. Science Fiction, Part 1 (1945-1974: Fordism). In *New Boundaries in Political Science Fiction,* ed. Donald M. Hassler and Clyde Wilcox, 115–144. Columbia: University of South Carolina Press.

CHAPTER 3

"There Is No War, There Is Only Harvest": Diplomatic Realpolitik and Combat Gameplay in *Mass Effect*

On the brink of what he presciently anticipated to be a coming century of apocalyptic total war, the scientific romancer H.G. Wells introduced a slim manual on miniature wargames, *Little Wars* (1913), with a biomedical analogy to immunization. Wells framed wargames as a "homeopathic remedy" to the devastation of modern war and its "embarrassment of every gracious, bold, sweet, and charming thing". By inoculating players against both the strategic pleasures and the brutal realities of future combat, the gamification of military war, Wells argues, can be pursued in a spirit of dissident deterrence of its real-world equivalent. In light of the gore-splattered commercial dominance of the so-called shooter genre of videogames today, from its popular inception in the space-marine combat of *Doom* (1993) through the endless iterations of the *Call of Duty* franchise (2003–2022), such an argument for virtual wargaming as a wholesome preemption of real-world martial aggression, and not merely blatant tools of militaristic propaganda, may strike many gamers today as flimsy.

While there seems to be no reason to quibble with a basic interpretation of the shooter genre, at its most bloodthirsty, as glamorizing war, this chapter wishes to critically update Wells's argument for certain instances of military SF in the simulated combat and dense narratives of diplomatic realpolitik found in contemporary videogames. The chapter contends in particular that the sophisticated space opera of *Mass Effect* engages its players in its own peculiar brand of blistering satire of modern war. This

© The Author(s), under exclusive license to Springer Nature Switzerland AG 2023
J. Winter, *BioWare's Mass Effect*, Palgrave Science Fiction and Fantasy: A New Canon,
https://doi.org/10.1007/978-3-031-18876-3_3

satire attacks many of the ideological justifications for modern warfare, including political vigilantism, violent torture tactics, neo-missionary economic colonialism, and the spirit of crusading moral adventurism that sadly also informs the cynical statecraft and political machinations of its early twenty-first-century cultural and historical context.[1] In the last analysis, the *Mass Effect* series presents a dark, cyberpunk-inflected future dominated by predatory flows of corporate inequality—as well as utopian ruptures of such a bleak status quo—and military violence, force, and coercion seem to be bound up with the scientific extraction of mineral resources, the industrial exploitation of people, and the accumulation of capital by the techno-elite, in a vast socio-economic condition analogous to what the Reapers label cycles of "harvest".

In the "Leviathan" Downloadable Content (DLC) supplement to *Mass Effect 3*, for instance, the deep history of the Reapers is traced to a near-extinct species called the leviathans, a massively scaled cuttlefish-like species of extraordinary sapience. In the narrative, Shepard encounters one of the few living leviathans that were once a dominant force in the galaxy but that have mysteriously gone into hiding. Shepard attempts to recruit the species as a pivotal war asset against the Reapers. In an oceanic abyss, the leviathan telepathically explains that hundreds of millions of years ago its species unshackled the Reapers, and their synthetic superintelligence, programming the entities with the hubristic imperative to efficiently preserve organic life over the vastness of eons and across the galaxy. This imperative was not altruistically pursued out of benevolent intentions but rather manifested the underlying colonial-capitalist design of the leviathans who viewed themselves as superior galactic caretakers and alien overlords, demanding "tribute" from their myriad client species. The newly created synthetic Reapers, though, perversely determined that preservation of the infinite variety of life could only be achieved by a periodic culling or

---

[1] It is precisely this perhaps too easily overlooked political reading of *Mass Effect* that struck many commentators as the source of a spectacular gaffe, when on April 4, 2016, Donald Trump tweeted the video of a supporter that juxtaposed images of protestors, bridges collapsing, and rows of derelict houses, to soaring bald eagles, Trump speeches, and the moon landing. Over these ham-fisted America-first propagandistic images dialogue from the big bad of the *Mass Effect* series, the Illusive Man, as voiced by Martin Sheen, calls out for the need for a messianic hero to fight back against vague threats that show "humanity is under attack". Electronic Arts immediately issued a copyright claim, and the video was deleted from Trump's Twitter account. Nevertheless, the hilarious irony that the voice of this fan-generated agitprop belongs to the Illusive Man, an unscrupulous, power-hungry tyrant-manqué of a figure, was certainly lost on the Trump campaign.

"harvest"; the Reapers therefore proceeded to genocidally wipe out any self-destructive advanced species and artificially reassemble their physical husks into zombified soldiers in an effort to test their genetic-evolutionary fitness data. When Shepard asks for military aid in the climactic struggle against the Reapers in *Mass Effect 3*, the leviathan initially balks and refers to this brutal culling, saying, "there is no war, there is only harvest". Depending in part on whether the player chooses to be a paragon or renegade, it is up to the player to prove to the leviathan of this galactic future history that there is a utopian alternative to such a cynical calculus.

This overarching space-opera narrative of Reaper-induced harvest also dynamically shapes the combat gameplay of the *Mass Effect* series. The combat mechanics of *Mass Effect* have proven massively popular in part because they are "easy to learn but hard to master", a ludic design feature that Jesper Juul theorizes as "emergent gameplay" (76). In emergent gameplay, a relatively simple set of rule-bound constraints in a game unpredictably generates a bewildering tactical and strategic complexity of interesting player choices. In *Mass Effect*, the ludic design of combat gameplay is most apparent in the customization of character skill levels and weapons, the non-fictive artificially intelligent programming of the non-player characters (NPCs), and the intricate integration of level design and narrative. Unlike less narrative-driven shooter games in which the gameplay frequently legitimates the untrammeled use of military force, *Mass Effect* stresses the strategic ethical and moral value of diplomatic realpolitik, even in the frenetic throes of the combat gameplay. This diplomacy-oriented narrative branching continually affords players immersed in combat with critical opportunities to reflect on and reimagine the utopian possibilities of tentative peacekeeping, the fostering of unstable alliances, and the delicate moderation of militant xenophobic factions.[2]

---

[2] The operating assumption of this chapter is that a player can read the politics of the *Mass Effect* series as an insightful allegory for our times. Naturally, mapping oppressive or liberating politics, or the absence of ideological positioning thereof, onto a commercial videogame entertainment is a fraught critical enterprise, as pioneering videogame scholar Espen Aarseth influentially argued in a discussion of the ancestors of games like *Mass Effect*, namely, text-based role-playing adventure games, interactive fiction, and multi-user dungeons (MUDs). Aarseth argues that the politics and the ludonarrative mechanics of a videogame should not be hastily ascribed to a monolithic ideological position, but he does also embrace the critical potential for videogames to transform how cultural politics operate in mediascapes where "the user has the ability to transform the text into something the instigator of the text could not foresee or plan for" (164). For an example of an academic position that disagrees with me, see Voorhees who, contra the position of this chapter, argues that "the games in the *Mass Effect* series function as cultural technologies that legitimate neoliberal multiculturalist ideology" (268).

The trope of a people-harvesting superintelligence is by no means unique to the *Mass Effect* universe, of course. A signal trope of post-singularity space opera—or gonzo space adventures about abundant virtual markets operated at vast scales by unimaginably advanced artificial intelligences—as Steven Shaviro explains by way of explicating the novels of Charles Stross, is optimizing the revenue streams of capitalist business and commercial interests, despite the imperative to "push their mania for accumulation to the point of implosion and extinction" (111). The cyberpunk-inflected expansions of virtual markets depicted in *Mass Effect* certainly follow the irrational exuberance of this logic, as fabulously sophisticated, techno-libertarian enclaves built on turbulent, risk-prone speculation continually threaten to bring about societal collapse under the overbearing weight of a material economic base of corrosive, rampant inequality. As evidence of the fiercely satirical mode of its narrative, not only does the videogame story world of *Mass Effect* frequently portray a woefully neglected wretched underclass living out harsh futures of extreme misery, but the narrative eternally returns to a disturbing fixation on the sinister operations of shadowy corporations often infiltrated by Reaper indoctrination, including the companies Cerberus, Binary Helix, Conatix Industries, the Elkoss Combine, and the Sirta Foundation.

Over the course of the three original games, ruthless corporations variously engage in corrupt biotech and artificial-intelligence experiments, conduct genocidal private military contracting, smuggle narcotics and illicit pharmaceuticals, manage deregulated prisons, traffic in sexual slavery, xenophobically screen refugees, and profiteer in arms manufacturing. As such, the corporations of *Mass Effect* are very much realistic, nuanced redactions of the melodramatic villainous pirates and gangsters that populated pulp-era space opera, such as the nefarious Boskonian cartel in E.E. "Doc" Smith's Lensmen series. The gritty, noirish tinge of the diplomatic realpolitik in particular undermines the progressive alibi explicitly endorsed in traditional space opera that a benevolent, heroic military and economic hierarchy promises to eugenically cleanse the universe of unregenerate evildoers. This dark and brooding vision of a corporation-dominated future marked by unregulated technological expansion perhaps contributed to what many vocal, avid fans felt was an overly downbeat and even—depending on the player's choices—outright miserabilist ending for *Mass Effect 3*.

In a systematic study conducted by Jacqueline Burgess and Christian M. Jones of 70,052 posts on "*ME3* Suggested Changes Feedback Thread:

Spoilers Allowed" hosted on BioWare's *Mass Effect* forums immediately following the release of the third game, it is clearly demonstrated that many avid players felt the ending of the original trilogy was a letdown and did not provide a win epic enough to sate their extremely whetted consumer appetites. On the forum, players vented their frustration that the ending of the series variously robbed them of player agency and customization options, lacked emotional closure, introduced unexplained or unjustified plot developments, and failed to deliver narrative significance. One major point of intense disappointment in these comments, Burgess and Jones show, was "rather than just stopping the Reapers, players wanted to be able to create a situation where Shepard and the characters they felt they had developed relationships with were happy" (156). In other words, the more or less unhappy ending of the original trilogy came as a surprise to players who had become emotionally attached to what at times amounted to a nostalgic space-opera series that seemed to exude the giddy optimism and utopian promise reminiscent of pulp SF traditions.

Within weeks of the otherwise commercially successful release of *Mass Effect 3*, another poll on the BioWare forums revealed that 88% of thousands of respondents were unsatisfied with the at-best bittersweet ending of the game. A community of these disgruntled fans mounted petitions and campaigns on social media sites to encourage BioWare to release an extended edition with an alternate ending, eventually leading to one such DLC, with a new ending option, as well as later DLC releases, including "Citadel", which provided more narrative closure and sandwiched in a comic happy ending for gamers emotionally invested in the series. One fan-generated campaign that received the mainstream attention of being featured on news coverage devoted to the controversy, the "Retake *Mass Effect*" campaign, even went so far as to raise nearly one hundred thousand dollars for the charity Child's Play, which provides gaming equipment to children's hospitals. This crowd-sourced charitable donation came in the wake of the less noble-minded prank of delivering to the BioWare office hundreds of cupcakes, each dyed in red, blue, or green food coloring, but each consisting of the same flavor. The delicious irony of this cupcake stunt was that a chief grievance of the upset fandom was that the three narrative choices for the original ending in the game—the "Destroy", "Control", and "Synthesis" choices, respectively—resulted in a montage whose only significant differences were the death or survival of Shepard; an altered voice-over script; the appearance or disappearance of some characters in the final montage; and a red, blue, or green tint to the last image sequence.

Ben Lindbergh insightfully observes that—in an early case of an increasingly common phenomenon in consumer culture of what is now being called "fantitlement", a portmanteau of fan and entitlement—this tempest in a teapot that marked the reception history of *Mass Effect 3* stems from a design flaw not in the narrative gameplay per se, which actually thematically resolves many of the preoccupations of the videogame series with a more or less interesting set of choice-based scenarios. Rather the backlash of gamers with *Mass Effect 3* derives in large part from the limitations and affordances of the innovative videogame mechanics of the whole series to begin with. Unsatisfied gamers felt deprived of agency because the vast accumulation of small gameplay choices did not ultimately add up to a meaningful variation in the endgame. Lindbergh sums up that the problem derives from the fact that the gameplay of the series "provided the appearance of player sovereignty that exceeded what it offered in the end". In other words, the problem with the ending was not only that it was unexpectedly downbeat, but rather the ending also put into high relief that even videogames that provide a wealth of meaningful choices must inevitably circumscribe such player agency in what Ian Bogost would call the "procedural rhetoric" of the core game design.

Specifically, to explain the ending controversy with more depth, here is, briefly, the essential narrative climax of the game series. The ending in question involves Shepard helping to activate the Crucible, a dimly understood big dumb object hastily built by the Alliance based on ancient blueprints excavated in a last-ditch effort to defeat the Reapers. After battling an apocalyptic invasion of Reaper forces across a devastated London cityscape—perhaps in a knowing allusion to H.G. Well's seminal *The War of the Worlds* (1897)—Shepard and Admiral Anderson are beamed up by a relay into the Citadel overrun by a Reaper infection. In the hallucinatory final scenes on the infected Citadel, a severely wounded Shepard engages in combat with the fearsome henchman Kai Leng, dispatches the Illusive Man once and for all, manipulates the controls so the Crucible docks with the Citadel, and then encounters an anthropomorphic projection of the Citadel, or the central intelligence unit of the Reapers, referred to, in a fitting echo of *2001: A Space Odyssey* (1968), as "the Star-Child". The character is so named in *Mass Effect 3* because the virtual projection looks like a small boy Shepard saw killed during the invasion of Earth at the beginning of the game, a boy who has repeatedly haunted Shepard's

traumatized nightmares. While explaining that the impressive construction of the Crucible has made the Reapers conclude that the harvest
imperative is an inadequate solution to the problem of optimizing the
infinite longevity of organic species galaxy-wide, the Star-Child gives the
player a choice between initiating red, blue, or green energy waves
throughout the galaxy: (1) the red "Destroy" option would make the
Citadel destroy all synthetic intelligence in the galaxy; (2) the blue
"Control" option would upload Shepard's consciousness into the Reaper's
code, allowing Shepard to reform the programming of the artificial intelligence from within; (3) and the green "Synthesis" option would nano-
technologically fuse all organic and synthetic life into hybrid genetic forms.
As an appeasement to the backlash, the "Extended Cut" DLC added a
fourth option where Shepard refuses to make any decision at all, prioritiz-
ing the Bartleby-esque freedom not to choose between equally bad
options as a paramount value. As argued in the Introduction to this book,
these endings thematize multiple perspectives on the procedural rhetoric
of the videogame medium itself, evocatively extending the sublime technological terror and wonder variously evoked by the prospect of machinic
advancement in SF genre history.

While these diverse choices of either opposing, hybridizing with, or
commandeering technological progress may seem to depict fateful grand
finales to the flamboyant narrative of the series, the forking narrative paths
also undeniably seemed paltry to many players. A primary reason for this
understandable frustration can be traced to the fact that the gameplay
mechanics cease to matter once the final choice is made; instead, the game
merely presents a rapid series of animations and graphics that chart out
glimpses of how galactic history will now be transformed. Especially since
the last montage consists of many non-animated still shots, the fandom
community suspected that production of the final stages of the game was
rushed to market. On a more visceral level, gamers were also distressed by
the fact that there was no single obviously preferable choice among the
three endings, despite the fact that the game insistently emphasized the
importance of gamer agency, with each of the options often entailing some
grave consequences for a beloved character. For instance, if the player
chooses the "Destroy" option, even the unshackled AI that is Normandy's
ship computer, EDI, is snuffed out. Moreover, the bleak tragic sacrifice of
the player's Shepard character in most of the playthrough options likewise
reinforces a dire outcome that may have been previously assumed by the
player to be subject to eventual heroic change by the frequently touted

messianic power of the player's agency. In other words, the end disappointed many precisely because the lack of significant gameplay following the last major choice reinforces on a narrative and generic level there being no fantastic way out for the hardball politics, corrosive capitalism, and treacherous diplomacy that shaped the galaxy for the series, regardless of a player's valiant desire for meaningful choice and collaborative storytelling.

The controversy swirling around the ending to *Mass Effect 3* then rehearses the sizable extent to which gameplay matters. The variable outcomes of the gameplay mechanics interact with the narrative dynamics in a videogame to create an immersive experience of agency for the player. For instance, the gameplay experience of missions centering on Shepard's squad mate Garrus Vakarian, a member of the militaristic turian species, is especially revelatory of how precisely combat mechanics shape story worlds throughout the *Mass Effect* series. The gameplay of these Garrus-centered main and side missions reenacts the moral quagmire in the ludonarrative experience of *Mass Effect*, as the player deftly navigates issues of inequality, exploitation, and complacency endemic to the Turian Hierarchy. As the Codex explains, the bureaucratic organization of the Turian Hierarchy is a heavily regimented and disciplined system of governance that worships a meritocracy of valor, civic-mindedness, and gung-ho self-sacrifice. In this capacity, the Turian Hierarchy simultaneously embodies a critical collective and individualistic impulse to counteract the deregulated corporate malfeasance, graft, and corruption that plagues the galaxy, much in tune with the superheroic missions of said space police popular in pulp space opera. Yet the aggressively militant turians did not begin to flourish as a species until they uplifted the volus as a client race. And the squat, suited volus are themselves a hyper-capitalist merchant species known for their high-tech cultural mastery of sophisticated corporate finance and banking.[3]

[3] On the one hand, the Turian Hierarchy enforces a bureaucracy of law and order that can be violently reactionary in its collusion with such aggressively competitive business interests and corporate power. This hegemonic fusion of corporate and governmental forces very much allegorizes the transnational flow of neoliberal capitalism today. On the other hand, the Turian Hierarchy embodies an honor-driven, duty-bound ethos dedicated to the collective curtailing of individual self-interest and mercenary exploitation. This narrative representation of the Turian Hierarchy hinges on the interplay between mindless conformism (law and order) and civic responsibility (vigilantism); this binary can oppositely be conceived as the struggle between anarchic difference (neoliberal capitalism) and regulative sameness (government regulation). The interplay can, for instance, be readily viewed in the turian facial tattoos that indicate their specific planetary group belonging and date back to the imperial consolidation of turian history called the Unification War. A lone wolf turian without any facial tattoos is automatically treated with suspicion and disdain by the group-oriented facially marked members of its species.

The hostility Garrus nurtures for the ineffective Citadel Security Services (C-Sec) bureaucracy has an oedipal tinge since his father, Castis Vakarian, is an exemplary by-the-books C-Sec officer. As the characterization of Garrus oscillates between the renegade pursuit of extreme justice and the paragon disavowing of vigilante violence, the turian maverick repeatedly lashes out at the bureaucratic red tape and conformist rule-mongering of diplomatic yes-men and milquetoast go-betweens. These obstructionists take various forms in the overarching narrative, from obsequious civil servants and middle-management functionaries who belong to the Turian Hierarchy, to the C-Sec space-station police, to the Alliance Council that facilitates the rogue Spectre black-ops agents and cultivates plausible deniability of the Reaper threat, to the criminal element on the mining city Omega and its slumlords, and finally to the private military contractor organization called Cerberus. In the first *Mass Effect*, Shepard first meets Garrus in the turian's capacity as a hard-boiled detective for the C-Sec Office; Shepard recruits the turian for the mission, as Garrus from the beginning suspects his narrative foil, another turian Spectre agent, Saren Arterius, of going rogue, despite receiving misguided protection from the Citadel Council. Garrus breaks the turian chain of command by openly complaining about his supervisor Executor Pallin to the human military hero Shepard he has just met, expressing his desire to "bring [Saren] down" because of a hunch that "rubs him the wrong way". During the combat mission involving Shepard's investigation into Fist, a double-crossing underling of Saren, Garrus peremptorily shoots in the head one of Fist's gang who has taken a hostage. Despite eventually recruiting Garrus for the mission to take Saren down, in the heat of battle a paragon Shepard upbraids Garrus for his hot-headedness, shouting at him "what were you thinking?" From the introduction of the character, then, Garrus moralistically denounces the status quo of diplomatic acquiescence as untenable, while at the same time clearly being too easily triggered into reactionary, proto-fascist vengeance.

Shepard can learn about Garrus's rebellious streak in the first *Mass Effect* during private chats on the Normandy. Then, on a personal-assignment combat mission, Shepard can help a vengeance-obsessed Garrus track down a mad scientist, the salarian Dr. Saleon, who escaped from C-Sec authorities after cloning organs to sell on the black market, grotesquely using his patients' own bodies as incubation chambers. On board the eerie MSV Fedele, Shepard and Garrus search for Dr. Saleon while periodically taking cover in a maze of cargo crates and corridors, shooting down zombie-like test patient NPCs as they erratically attack. Once Dr. Saleon is discovered during combat, in a conversational exchange, the player can allow Garrus to repay brute force with more of the same. Alternately, Dr. Saleon can be taken into custody to await trial and a possible technicality-contingent avoidance of punishment. However, even if a player chooses to spare Dr. Saleon, the ungrateful scientist resists arrest and then dies in the ensuing combat gameplay of a firefight. When the level has been completed, Garrus then understandably asks a paragon Shepard what the point was of not immediately executing the criminal. The paragon Shepard contends that regardless of the consequences, the moral high ground of such life-and-death decisions is never worth sacrificing. Near the end of the first *Mass Effect*, Garrus indeed confesses in a private chat with Shepard on the Normandy that he has realized the delusive error of his ways and that his bloodthirsty crusades against existing bureaucratic authorities were driven in no small measure by his petty need to be vindicated as a superior individual. While *Mass Effect* does not endorse complicity with a potentially corrupt system of governance and policing, the development of Garrus's moral arc emphasizes his gradual valuing of diplomatic patience and guarded tact over brute force when seeking justice, which militates against the default dynamic of shooter videogames that tend to fetishize adrenaline-fueled combat as the panacea for pervasive societal ills.

In *Mass Effect 2*, Garrus is re-introduced into the narrative during a combat mission on Omega, an ancient alien space station carved out of a hollowed-out asteroid shaped like an atomic mushroom cloud. Much like the bright, clean, and legalistic world of Illium, Omega is an asari-led anarchic, right-libertarian enclave, but unlike the bright and shining Illium, Omega is a dark city ridden with strife, squalor, and pollution and ruled over by fractious, marauding gangs of rival mercenaries. Omega neatly illustrates the frequently overlooked notion that the utopian freedoms of right-libertarian ideology also guide what Fredric Jameson calls "various xenophobic and racist group practices" (8). After meeting with the informal asari ruler of Omega, the so-called Pirate Queen Aria T'Loak, Shepard receives the information that the three major mercenary groups—the Blue Suns, Eclipse, and Blood Pack—are planning a concerted mission to assassinate Archangel, a slum-dwelling vigilante who has been extra-judicially executing mercenaries. Ostensibly arriving in the Kima District of Omega for the mercenary assault, Shepard has the ulterior motive of recruiting the skilled sniper Archangel for the suicide attack on the Reaper-indoctrinated

Collectors. The figure of Archangel is a dubious bundle of contradictions whose ruthless vigilantism reveals both an unnerving equivalency with the existing authority of private military contractors—the player as Shepard, a Cerberus agent, must be included here—and an inchoate desire for radical justice secured only by dismantling the corrupt balance of powers.

The ludic combat gameplay in this Archangel mission mirrors the player's divided loyalties, split between the conflicting poles of anarchic violence and messianic justice. The apparent switching of sides during the mission blurs the binary between the player as either a justice-seeking vigilante or an opportunistic soldier of fortune. When Shepard arrives at the Kima District, a dialogue cut-scene exchange involves Shepard and two crewmembers impersonating a new mercenary recruit and reporting to a free-lance batarian named Sergeant Cathka in order to move beyond the barriers to where Archangel has barricaded himself. A renegade interrupt option allows Shepard to stab Cathka in the back with an electric welder, thus preventing the mercenary from fully repairing a gunship that Shepard will have to battle later in the mission. Whether or not this interrupt option is chosen, Shepard and crew are accepted as legitimate mercenaries by enemy non-player characters. This makes the combat gameplay different than in other battles because the enemies proceed cautiously into the building to a locked door, instead of immediately taking cover and shooting at Shepard. If the player chooses to fire on the mercenaries, perhaps shooting one of them in the back, then the charade is over, a frazzled mercenary alerts his comrades of the double-cross by shouting that Shepard is "with Archangel", and NPCs now fight the player while hacking the locked door to ambush Archangel.

Once the mercenaries are defeated in combat, and Shepard enters the now unlocked second-floor room, a cinematic cut-scene shows Archangel removing his helmet and it is revealed that the legendary vigilante of the Omega slums has in fact been the player's old crewmember Garrus all along. During the cut-scene exchange where Garrus and Shepard strategize how to escape, the gameplay allows the player to briefly control a sniper scope that Garrus hands Shepard to survey the situation. The player can view robotic scouts infiltrating the building; as Shepard now seeks to rescue an old friend, the player must duck, roll, take cover, and shoot down these non-sentient robotic scouts followed by heavy mechs, and the narrative morality of Shepard's actions become less duplicitous than earlier in the mission.[4] The added gameplay dynamic of a bar appearing on the bottom of the screen indicating Garrus's slowly deteriorating vital signs also intensifies the sense that the mission has become less self-interested and more multilateral.

The techno-utopian, right-libertarian power fantasy of the scenario, however, is not completely effaced, since Shepard must still righteously gun down mercenaries, including the leader of the Eclipse gang, the salarian Jaroth, who nurses a vengeful grudge against Garrus for slaying his brother. Shepard must also fend off the krogan battlemaster and Blood Pack leader, Garm, and his minions, in order to shutter the doors on the bottom floor from further incursions. While Garrus is gloating over the deaths of these mercenary kingpins, he is taken down by a hail of rounds from a flying helicopter-like gunship operated by the batarian Blue Suns leader, Tarak. Once Shepard disposes of this gunship and the last remaining mercenary leader, perhaps ushering in a brief respite from merciless carnage for the oppressed denizens of Omega, the player ferries a physically and emotionally scarred Garrus back to the med bay on the Normandy.

The optional narrative arc to foreground Garrus's gradual redemption from his obsession with vigilante justice undercuts the rationalization of violence endemic to the shooter genre of videogames. In Garrus's loyalty mission in *Mass Effect 2*, titled "An Eye for an Eye", Garrus enlists Shepard in hunting down one of his former turian partners, Lantar Sidonis, who betrayed Garrus to a mercenary group, leading to the death of ten of his teammates in an ambush. This subplot strips Garrus of his ordinary

---

[4] Depending on the player-chosen difficulty settings, the emergent complexity of the combat mechanics here can also be quite challenging in terms of mastering combat and resource management, as the player must learn how to play the game through staggered trial and error, and most likely many character deaths and frequent saving. This chapter only concentrates on gameplay integral to narrative; however, to give a sense of the complexity a competent player of the shooter aspects of *Mass Effect* must skillfully maneuver, here is a quick, incomplete list of hand-eye coordination and split-second decisions necessary for the combat gameplay that do not simply consist of button mashing and mindless mayhem. Players must target a reticule at enemies and fire their weapons, run for cover, shoot suppressive fire, melee, flank, strategize reloading opportunities, and conserve weapons and ammunition. Players must also toggle through and deploy appropriate resources, tracking one's health bar and selecting when to use special moves, such as healing, biotics, cryonics, and incineration, according to a player's chosen military specialization. Players also track enemies on the radar, orient their position according to the level map, control the positioning of their squad, and interact with environmental objects by blowing up containers or salvaging more health and ammunition.

altruistic and duty-bound motivations of ridding the galaxy of its crime-infested bad actors, instead underscoring a stark desire for brutal vengeance. Following Garrus's lead, Shepard tracks a volus reportedly named Fade through the Neon Markets on the Citadel; this volus, though, turns out to be a pawn of the actual racketeer responsible for securing Sidonis's forged identity information, which he has used to disappear. The real criminal mastermind is the human Harkin, a disgruntled former C-Sec officer introduced in the first *Mass Effect* game, who now serves as a narrative foil for Garrus, given that Harkin's sleazy grievances against bureaucratic bloat only mask his own venal incompetence.

In the first part of the combat mission, Shepard and Garrus, plus an additional squad mate, press past the gates of a warehouse in hot pursuit of Harkin, who is defended by a small army of Blue Sun troopers, commandos, corporate-manufactured robots, and giant mechs. In its forward movement toward the deep recesses of the warehouse and Harkin's office, the level design of the combat mission highlights the corruption, black-market smuggling, and graft at the vicious economic and infrastructural base of the Citadel's flourishing future city. The unscrupulous Harkin's capital in the galactic underworld means that in addition to enemies wielding rockets and heavy artillery attacking the zig-zagging player, robots hide in shipping containers, mechs are dropped from cranes, office windows conceal vision, transport platforms need to be raised, and Shepard must swipe forged IDs to pass security clearance. The bewildering chaos of shipping crates scattered throughout the level also creates convenient cover for Shepard and team, frequently disrupting the lines of sight of the enemy NPCs. A skilled player will not only scavenge the med-gel, heavy ammo, credits, and iridium resources ready for the taking but also direct squad members to concentrate on powerful commandos, explode containers to conserve ammo, and use biotic special powers against unarmored troopers.

Once Harkin is cornered in his office, a cinematic cut-scene with dialogue-wheel options ensues, and regardless of whether the player has been leaning toward a paragon or renegade playthrough, they will need to intervene to stop Garrus from crushing a prostrate Harkin who complains that giving up Sidonis will hurt his forgery business. When Garrus quips, "you know what else is bad for business, a broken neck", Shepard prevents the situation from becoming extra-judicially lethal. Only the paragon player, though, will stop Garrus from shooting Harkin in the kneecap to slow his escape from the C-Sec authorities en route. Despite Garrus's understandable frustration with official law enforcement only colluding with treacherous business and corporate interests, the game encourages players to diplomatically talk Garrus down from the brink of being irremediably vicious. Even in disagreeable renegade mode, Shepard will question the double standards of Garrus's moral absolutism and offer to negotiate a peaceful resolution to the conflict between Sidonis and himself. Garrus will reluctantly acquiesce.

In the ensuing conservation with Sidonis, Shepard will stand between Garrus and his target, the interactive scene cutting back and forth between the conversation and the scope on Garrus's sniper scope, its shot repeatedly blocked by the back of Shepard's head. Despite Garrus's protestations overheard through Shepard's earpiece, the paragon player can repeatedly choose the "keep talking" dialogue option, which prevents Garrus from shooting Sidonis. The conversation with Sidonis also reveals that the kidnapped Sidonis betrayed Garrus's team only under extreme, life-threatening duress, an eventuality that makes the self-righteous pose in Garrus's shouting of "coward" ring hollow. Without offering an apology for systemic injustice and pervasive corruption, the game makes the player engage in a circumspect weighing of moral and narrative ambiguities, emphasizing the need for nuanced deliberation in a fashion quite opposed to the standard untroubled applauding of militarized violence popular in jingoistic wargames. Choosing the paragon path in this side mission not only completes a redemptive narrative arc for Garrus but also opens up a strategic advantage for Shepard in the suicide mission that ends the game, as it allows Garrus to valiantly command a second squad through the Collector base without dying in the process.

Garrus's lumpen vigilantism, and its recourse to the-ends-justify-the-means rationalizations, makes him ethically and politically no different from the bureaucratic authorities against which he ritually rails. His complicated moral redemption therefore also suggests a utopian alternative to the periodic singularity-driven collapse of the ruling classes in the galactic megahistory of *Mass Effect*. The ancient AI uprising narrative of the Reapers, after all, marks an existential cosmic battle between synthetic and organic life which the mercenary gangs, drug syndicates, sex-trafficking rings, and gambling cartels of the galaxy ditheringly ignore. In the allegory of neoliberal capital that this mechanized threat reenacts, a resistant and dissident multitude challenges the nomadic flows of an empire that both shapes and reflects the corrupt culture it reproduces. Significantly, at one point in *Mass Effect 2*, a salarian scientist, Mordin, contrasts the "culturally dead" aspects of the Reaper-dominated Collectors to the artistic creativity of organic species by enthusiastically singing an updated libretto to Gilbert and Sullivan's comic opera *The Pirates of Penzance*. In one narrative thread, Mordin even sings the patter song before his heroic suicidal death as he cures the krogan genophage: "I am the very model of a scientist salarian,/I've studied species turian, asari, and batarian!" The recursive wit of this routine cannily recontextualizes the Victorian stage-musical's burlesque of the British empire for its own radically estranged space-operatic story world. The ruthless machinations of the criminal underworld of smugglers, slavers, pirates, hackers, assassins, arms dealers, and mafioso parallel the more outwardly salubrious, yet no less complicit operations of the bankers, merchants, ambassadors, generals, and ordinary citizens. The entire variegated spectrum of social strata is an indirect function of the sinister, mechanized cycles of harvest, that is, the post-Singularity accumulations of commercial markets and corporate free enterprise anchored in the spectacular acceleration of futuristic technological progress.

In the DLC to *Mass Effect 3* called "Omega", the utopian prospect of democratic governance offers an alternative that promises to subvert the ideological authorization of bellicose regimes that pervades the shooter genre. Again, this acerbic satirical subversion is experienced by the player directly through the dynamic integration of narrative-based diplomacy and combat gameplay. The asari Pirate Queen, Aria T'Loak, who Shepard previously collaborated with to recruit Archangel in *Mass Effect 2*, requests aid to recapture Omega, which has been invaded and occupied by the private military contractor Cerberus. As per the morally compromised diplomatic realpolitik of the game, in exchange for Shepard's aid, the underworld gangster promises to lend troops, ships, and resources as war assets in Shepard's fight against the apocalyptic Reaper menace. During their preparatory secret meeting to discuss the retaliatory assault on the occupied Omega, Aria awkwardly positions herself as the liberator of the oppressed—she declares that she wants Omega to be restored to its status as a libertarian enclave where the outlaw denizens know "their lives are theirs"—and as deposed tyrant seeking to regain her "ruthless" rule with an "iron fist".

The ludic game design of this scenario is ironically winked at when the genius strategist and free-lancing general in charge of Cerebus's occupying forces on Omega, Oleg Petrovsky, once Shepard has deactivated Omega's cannons, is visually depicted as a contemplative chess master, toppling an enemy castle with the diagonal slash of a bishop, muttering over the game board to himself, "so it begins". This cut-scene follows an earlier holographic parlay where a paragon or renegade Shepard can engage in either canny brinksmanship or tactful rapprochement. Indeed, as the combat level first begins, during a conversational exchange, the player is given Shepard's first ludonarrative choice. Shepard can either lead the ground assault or follow Aria; this minor choice determines the game state of whether Shepard follows Aria as an NPC, or whether Aria follows Shepard. While leading the charge might only add mild difficulty to the gameplay, given the elegance of the level design, the choice neatly underscores the underlying thematic question of democratic leadership versus authoritarian rule that will insistently recur throughout the level.

The mission, then, develops a significant plot complication when the player as Shepard, en route to a rendezvous point with Aria's forces, can click on crates with red graffiti tags indicating the presence of the Talon resistance gang. Aria explains what this local symbol means to Shepard, and the player neutrally comments that the resistance could be "useful" to her assault. Aria complains, though, that the gang used to "deface" her "property" too; the jealously proprietary attitude toward Omega implied in this remark also can be overheard in Aria's shouts during combat that "Omega is mine!" The seemingly thin line between narrative foils Aria and Oleg can be especially chilling to paragon players as they confront a brand-new NPC enemy, the Rampart Mechs, while following the green holographic signs on openable doors in the maze of rooms and corridors on the way to the rendezvous point. The robots serve as ad-hoc law enforcement that brutally police the obstreperous civilian population on Omega. The player is repeatedly led to question whether Aria likewise has the best interest of the citizens of Omega in mind during and after the assault. This question is especially unnerving since Rampart Mechs are formidable opponents even against a highly skilled player during combat gameplay. These robots are quick-moving, protected by strong force fields; they self-destruct their shotguns in explosions that can damage the player and are capable of lethal lunges of close combat explained by the Codex as an overclocked "hunter-killer" mode. The player must be tactically smart, deploying headshots from powerful sniper rifles from a distance, using the appropriately advanced shotgun for close combat, and deploying incendiary ammunition, or, most cleverly of all, using a leveled-up sabotage skill to hack the robots and temporarily convert them into allied combatants.

On the way to Aria's bunker, Shepard and Aria then stumble on Nyreen Kandros, a female turian who Aria did not know was still on Omega and who seems to have some unfinished romantic history with the asari crime boss. Like Garrus, Nyreen is an outlier to the Turian Hierarchy at large; however, unlike Garrus, Nyreen does not upbraid the hypocrisy of the turian rigid insistence on bureaucratic law and order so much as rebel against the exclusionary xenophobia of her species. For Nyreen is a rare turian gifted with biotic abilities, and the Turian Hierarchy therefore sidelines her potentially meteoric military career as a result. It is difficult not to read Nyreen's backstory as allegorizing issues of gender and sexuality in the male-dominated military hierarchy of today, especially as Nyreen migrates to Omega and becomes erotically entangled with Aria precisely to fulfill her otherwise spoiled potential. And unlike Garrus, Nyreen herself is not severely morally compromised, maintaining a turian code of strict ethics in her newly realized devotion to helping the underclass citizens of Omega.

In a conversational exchange between Aria and Shepard, Nyreen, as a bitter ex-lover, therefore, spares Aria no harsh words, repudiating the Pirate Queen's "moral bankruptcy", her "itching for revenge", and her willingness to "carve a bloody path" through civilian collateral in her desperate attempt to regain control of Omega. When it is gradually revealed that Nyreen has been hiding from Aria since the turian has assumed leadership of the Talon gang, it is clear that Nyreen has carefully guided the transformation of the profit-seeking mercenaries into political freedom fighters. The player as Shepard is now presented with a moral double bind that shapes the gameplay of the level. On the one hand, Shepard can show trust in and sympathy for Nyreen's cause, rejecting what Nyreen characterizes as Aria's "power trip" and her unscrupulous willingness to use civilians as "cannon fodder". On the other hand, Shepard can support Aria's emergency actions, recognizing the instrumental value of what even Nyreen understands to be Aria's charismatic disposition, and the way "this beautiful fierce creature" is committed to risk everything in her all-consuming obsessions, and therefore can crucially help Shepard in the overarching goal of defeating the Reaper threat.

The irresolvable nature of this double bind comes through in the combat gameplay when Shepard and team encounter the new enemy NPCs called "Adjutants". These Reaper-modified monstrosities are horrific; they shamble about with distended pulsating brains bulging out from skull-less heads, blue beady eyes shining in the dark, and slimy tentacles protruding from their face. And the Adjutants wreak terrifying havoc on the already ravaged population of Omega. Aria criticizes Nyreen for showing trepidation in her battles with Adjutants, and Nyreen admits she is deathly afraid of these abominations. Beyond their grotesquerie, what scares Nyreen seems to be that the Adjutants are inexplicable politically and ethically; they are not easily categorized into the existing conceptual schemas of official public discourse, and Nyreen's utopian aims for democratic reform on Omega fail to cohere when confronted with this outside menace. Given the larger threat of Reaper invasion, strategic cooperation with Aria, and against Oleg and the Reaper-infiltrated organization of Cerberus, seems called for. Yet this realpolitik diplomacy seems to eclipse the democratically minded Nyreen's impetus to "fight for a better world" on Omega and to speak as a "voice of the people". Similarly, the charging, leaping, and evading movements as well as the biotic immobilizing projectiles of the Adjutants also disrupt the combat mechanics the player has likely mastered by this point in the game, especially the cover-and-shoot tactics that have proven effective in most battles. Instead of establishing such stationary outpost positions, players must themselves dodge, duck, and roll more erratically, deploying weapons and biotics at a safe distance to avoid singularity projectiles that drain necessary shields and close-range lunge attacks.

Nyreen ultimately overcomes her paralyzing fear of Adjutants but at a tragic cost. This outcome suggests that perhaps a utopian reconciliation between small-scale reform on Omega and megahistorical galaxy saving can be managed by the adept player. In a trap carefully laid by the mastermind Oleg, deep in the mining infrastructure of Omega, the moral complexity of gameplay reaches a climax when Shepard must choose between powering down a reactor immediately, which will cut off life support for thousands of civilians on Omega, or more patiently rerouting the power to make sure the reactor only eliminates Oleg's force fields that impede Aria's assault. If you kill the life support and hit the big red overload button, Shepard receives significant renegade points, Nyreen reasonably loses confidence in Shepard's moral decency, and Aria is practically gleeful. If the player reroutes the reactor power, despite the clear and present danger of mission failure with Aria and Nyreen being on the brink of death at the hands of Reaper Mechs, then Nyreen praises Shepard's moral grace under pressure and Aria castigates the player for having a "soft heart". Interestingly, if you have chosen to be an engineer in your original character selection, you can immediately reroute power and avoid the interruption scenes of moral dilemma, thus evading alienating either Aria or Nyreen.

Since Nyreen will nobly sacrifice herself by blowing up a biotic bomb in a frenzy of Adjutants during the climactic assault on the Afterlife night-club, the narrative consequences of the level revolve around whether paragon Shepard helps disprove Oleg's shrewd prediction that Aria will never change, and that Aria's governance of the station will never ameliorate the mass squalor of Omega. Attempting to play psychological mind games with Shepard, Oleg echoes Nyreen when he predicts that as ruler Aria will only ever burnish her ego in the service of "the greater glory of Aria". The final moral choice presented to Shepard reinforces the significance of the interplay of gameplay and narrative in the level design, as Shepard saves Aria, who, in her rage-fueled grief over Nyreen's sacrifice, flings herself onto Oleg's last carefully sprung trap that shackles Aria to electro-magnetic restraints. The device is timed to kill Aria, and while waging battle against a hoard of Adjutants, and assorted other enemies, Shepard must destroy a series of generators to allow Aria to release periodic blasts of biotic shock-wave. These blasts inflict damage on the otherwise unbeatable mixture of challenging opponents. The vanguard character customization proves especially adept in this final showdown, provided the player takes advantage of biotic speed augmentation and the continual restoration of personal shield protection.

Regardless of the seemingly limitless multiplicity of specific combat tactics available to a player, the intersection of narrative and gameplay underscores Aria's pivotal role in the assault on Omega. The disturbing final moral choice to either strangle a surrendered Oleg or take the captured general in as a valuable information source in the fight against the Reapers will ultimately inform the rhetorical pitch of Aria's broadcast victory speech to Omega's citizens. Under the renegade playthrough, Aria will incite the mob to exact sadistic revenge against the remaining Cerberus infiltrators and vow to make Omega her exclusive "domain" again. As a special kink in this renegade climax, Aria can even passionately kiss Shepard as the culmination of their psychosexual alliance. Oppositely, under the paragon playthrough, Aria complains that she has been "infected like a disease" by Shepard's utopian ideals, and in the victory speech Aria urges that the people of Omega be merciful toward their defeated adversaries, voices a collective call for reform, and inspiringly concludes, "we may be bruised, but we are Omega". Just as in the midst of the chaotic carnage of the combat gameplay, Shepard can pause and choose to use precious medical resources to heal wounded soldiers while fighting, so Aria now seems to have manifested unexpected mercy and to have discovered a newfound respect for democratic coalitions. Likewise, in the end, despite Oleg's unconscionable war crimes, the narrative consequences of paragon Shepard's choices are driven home when Oleg is granted asylum by morally questionable Alliance officials, but a player will also be notified that Oleg provides vital assistance to the war effort and helps to destroy a Cerberus base.

Not only does *Mass Effect* as a series consistently avoid the glorification of martial combat characteristic of the shooter videogame, but it also shows that an unjust system of runaway disparities undergirds such violence and chaos. This chapter has argued that the unfolding of the diplomatic and deliberative narrative strands of the *Mass Effect* series repeatedly reinforces this coupling of narrative backstory with the combat mechanics of character customization, NPC interaction, and level design. Yet with remarkable consistency for such a team-scripted narrative continually co-authored by participant gamers in an act of collaborative storytelling, the procedural rhetoric of the *Mass Effect* series critically underscores the power of commodity exchange, the circulation of capital, and the machinations of commercial markets in the perpetuation of technologically sophisticated violence and elaborate shows of military force. In fact, despite the wide variety of multi-species rivalries in the videogame series, only shooter combat against the renegade machines of the Reapers is authorized as unequivocally morally justified in the grand narrative of the galactic future history.

References

Aarseth, Espen. 1997. *Cybertext.* Baltimore: John Hopkins University Press.

BioWare. 2007. *Mass Effect 1.* BioWare. PC/Mac/Consoles.

———. 2010. *Mass Effect 2.* BioWare. PC/Mac/Consoles.

———. 2012. *Mass Effect 3.* BioWare. PC/Mac/Consoles.

———. 2021. *Mass Effect: Legendary Edition.* BioWare. PC/Mac/Consoles.

Jameson, Fredric. 2005. *Archaeologies of the Future: The Desire Called Utopia and Other Science Fictions.* New York: Verso.

Juul, Jesper. 2005. *Half Real: Video Games Between Real Rulers and Fictional Worlds.* Cambridge: MIT Press.

Lindbergh, Ben. 2022. *Mass Effect 3* Foreshadowed Fandom's Divided Decade. *The Ringer*, March 4. https://www.theringer.com/2022/3/4/22961040/mass-effect-3-ending-legacy-backlash

Shaviro, Steven. 2009. The Singularity is Here. In *Red Planets: Marxism and Science Fiction*, ed. Mark Bould and China Miéville, 103–117. Middletown: Wesleyan University Press.

Voorhees, Gerald. 2012. Neo-liberal Multiculturalism in *Mass Effect*: The Government of Difference in Digital RPGs. In *Dungeons, Dragons, and Digital Denizens*, ed. Gerald Voorhees, Joshua Call, and Katie Whitlock, 259–277. New York: Continuum International Publishing Group.

CHAPTER 4

Embracing Eternity: FemShep, Queer Romance, and Diversity

Progressive members of the gaming community have heralded BioWare for showing that the representation of diverse viewpoints in videogames matters. This policy challenges the default status quo of the videogame industry, which has been known to unreflectively appeal to the exclusive demographic of the straight white male player. Especially given the estimable vocal talents of the performer Jennifer Hale, the ability to play as a heroic female avatar, the so-called FemShep option, strikes many gamers as more than a simple "re-skin". To these gamers, FemShep is a subversive leap of the imagination that contests the undeniable reality that "women still face an uphill struggle in gaining and excelling within leadership roles in real life" (Urquhart 2021). In contrast to the typically passive female characters in videogames, FemShep disrupts cisgendered, hetero-masculine norms in her role as a tough female supersoldier who is never a damsel in distress waiting to be rescued, even if the player chooses to make their FemShep a compassionate paragon.[1]

---

[1] Despite the fact that FemShep was an option from the first *Mass Effect* onward, it was not until the Collector's edition that FemShep was featured on promotional materials, which created an outcry from players who did not approve of the distinctive look of this official version. Tanja Sihvonen compellingly argues that this controversy stems from seminal collaborative storytelling affordances granted to player agency in the first place: "if the players' choice of creating the kinds of characters they want is taken away, or if they are too vigorously guided in the way of the developer company, a big part of the game's appeal seems to be lost".

J. Winter, *BioWare's Mass Effect*, Palgrave Science Fiction and Fantasy: A New Canon,
https://doi.org/10.1007/978-3-031-18876-3_4

Moreover, in addition to the player-customization choices for Shepard to be Black, Asian, or Latinx, the series also features several iconic non-player characters (NPCs) of color. This includes Shepard's mentor and superior officer, Captain David Anderson (voiced by Keith David), who videogame journalist Jason Guisao singles out as a "respectful" and "inspiring" representation of a complex, accomplished, empowered Black man.[2] And given the inclusion of gay, lesbian, and bisexual characters as well as the ability to romance these characters with a queer player avatar, Aubrey Livi, in 2017, offers this even-handed plaudit: "BioWare has made huge (if imperfect) strides regarding LGBTQ representation in its games over the past seventeen years". This groundbreaking commitment to enhancing the visibility of marginalized minority viewpoints resists the countervailing norms of misogyny, homophobia, and racism that have become virulent in videogame culture today. Prior to the release of *Mass Effect 3* in 2011, consumer backlash reached a belligerent pitch in the BioWare website forums as some disgruntled players argued against BioWare's campaign to spearhead more inclusive representation. In a carefully worded forum response on the gradual evolution of BioWare's response to such backlash, David Gaider, the writer and designer of BioWare's high-fantasy *Dragon Age* series, spoke out eloquently against the entitlement and privilege inherent in such insecurity. Speaking on behalf of the BioWare developers who remain decidedly "unconvinced" of the strident criticisms voiced by players who wish to exclude and marginalize different sexualities, genders, and races from future games, Gaider says: "you can write [inclusion of minority character options] off as 'political correctness' if you wish, but the truth is that privilege always lies with the majority ... [who are] so used to being catered to that they see the lack of catering as an imbalance" (qtd. in Kane 2011). In their dismantling of such entitled grievances, the BioWare designers and developers promote diversity as the logical outgrowth of the choose-your-own-adventure collaborative storytelling inherent in the series. For instance, Gaider has elsewhere testified that the deliberate hiring of women for the BioWare writing staff ensured the inclusion of female voices in the narrative development

---

[2] Drew Karpyshyn's novelizations—*Mass Effect: Revelation* (2007), *Mass Effect: Ascension* (2008), and *Mass Effect: Retribution* (2010)—focus on the backstory of David Anderson as he progresses from lieutenant to captain and develops a complicated romantic relationship with Dr. Kahlee Sanders who teaches at the Grissom Academy, the Alliance's school for young human biotics.

of games by "otherwise intelligent and liberal guys who are then shocked to find out they inadvertently offended a group that is quickly approaching *half of the gaming audience*" (qtd. in deWinter and Kocurek 2017, 67, emphasis in original).[3]

FemShep counters the default legacy of hard-body, sadistic masculinity as featured in the touchstone cinematic action roles performed by the likes of Arnold Schwarzenegger or Sylvester Stallone. In contrast, FemShep seems emphatically aligned with the rise of powerful female action heroes in cinema, what the critic Cora Kaplan has called the "Dirty Harriette" phenomenon, as best exemplified in the SF genre by the film icons Sarah Connor (Linda Hamilton) in *Terminator 2* (1991) and Ellen Ripley (Sigourney Weaver) in *Aliens* (1986). Although ultimately arguing that BioWare has not yet been progressive enough in its appeal to transgender and queer players, Amanda Philipps nevertheless expresses admiration for the stunning way the FemShep avatar "can execute the same muscular approaches to social interaction as BroShep [the fan designation for the male version of Shepard], headbutting armored aliens, carrying fallen comrades over her shoulders, and starting bar brawls" (143). Just as by operating a mechanical shipping loader exo-suit in *Aliens*, Weaver's Ripley deftly dismantles prevalent sexist assumptions about female physical incompetence, so FemShep, in the first *Mass Effect*, swiftly rebukes the unwanted advances of a corrupt ex-security officer, Harkin, who also happens to be a chauvinist pig. Apropos of nothing, Harkin calls FemShep "princess" and the player is provided a dialogue-wheel option to retort with a no-nonsense quip that puts the harasser in his place: "call me princess again and you'll be picking your teeth up off the floor".

As Phillips's analysis suggests, the *Mass Effect* series has nonetheless faced substantive critiques from not fully satisfied minority, female, and transgender-identified players and academic critics who feel these videogames have not yet been boldly inclusive enough in their reform-minded constructions of diverse identity viewpoints. A vibrant community of

[3] The mostly widely cited statistic is the yearly report from the Entertainment Software Association, which, as of the 2021 report, states that 45% of gamers identify as female. However, before glibly applying such a statistic to *Mass Effect*, it must be remembered that, according to the same report, 63% of these gamers overall testify that they play casual games such as *Solitaire* or *Tetris*, and the percentage of gamers overall who play mobile games on their smartphone is 57%. The percentage of female gamers who play an action or shooter game on a console or personal computer is therefore probably significantly lower than the 45% statistic.

players has arisen over the years to provide niche modifications, or "mods", to *Mass Effect* games, posting instructions online for how to change the existing code to the program. These modders endeavor to overcome the zealously cautious tendencies of high-profile entertainments like *Mass Effect* that result in the failure to provide fully diverse customizations of the player's identity, narrative, and romance options to the broadest range of audiences. This chapter will examine some of these ingenious, boundary-pushing mods as well as the fascinating representations provided by the unmodified videogame series itself for transformative visions of gender, sexuality, and race. The chapter will also discuss the attempt to diversify the representations of the *Mass Effect* universe beyond the videogames proper, particularly by award-winning SF writers N.K. Jemisin and Catherynne M. Valente in their *Mass Effect* novelizations.

Since the variable narrative experience of the *Mass Effect* series is very much a la carte, it should be noted that individual playthroughs, not to mention after-market mods, have been criticized as prone to reinforcing an incoherent "multiculturalist ideology" (Voorhees 2012, 259). The queer, nonwhite, and feminist narrative pathways discussed in this chapter, after all, are only some possible game options among myriad other collaborative storytelling alternatives. Players can just as easily choose to play through the *Mass Effect* series with the traditional customization options of a straight white male hero, opting to exclude the intrusion of alternative identities in their gameplay. However, even these players are confronted by various non-player characters of different ethnicities, genders, sexualities, and alien species; additionally, these players need to actively reject gay, lesbian, or bisexual romance options and other side-mission storylines that disrupt the ostensible objective neutrality of their putatively privileged hetero-masculine subject positions; and indeed, as we saw in the controversy in the *Mass Effect* website forums, some of the more aggrieved of the straight white male players have even publicly complained that receiving subtle romantic overtures from a non-hetero NPC was jarringly disruptive to their traditional gameplay.

Mass Effect played a small role in the so-called Gamergate controversy in which prominent feminist voices in the gamer community, such as Zoe Quinn, Anita Sarkessian, and Brianna Wu, received rape and death threats, sexual harassment, and "doxing" (the publishing of private information online) in a failed attempt to silence their criticism. In the episode "Body Language and the Male Gaze" from the video-essay series *Tropes* Versus *Women*, Anita Sarkessian inserts some graphics of the character Miranda from *Mass Effect* to explicate the prevailing unrealistic gendered norms in videogames whereby "motion-capture animation for female characters often make them look like they're walking down a runway at fashion show in stiletto heels, even when the characters are actually in combat situations". Then, visually quoting the notorious cut-scene of a gratuitous shot from *Mass Effect 2* that awkwardly accentuates Miranda's tightly clad buttocks in a scene of high drama, which was subsequently removed from the Legendary edition of the game, Sarkessian argues that such examples are symptomatic of how women are casually hypersexualized, objectified, and demeaned in videogames catering to heterosexual male audiences. For her trailblazing efforts in the *Tropes* Versus *Women* series, Sarkessian was repeatedly targeted online in waves of attacks that escalated into offline harassment, including the hacking of her personal information, bomb threats, canceled speaking appearances, and a criminal trial. These attacks corroborated in a sobering way the dire significance of her critique of the videogame industry as a potentially violent hypermasculine space.

A feminist and queer videogame culture has also, though, rallied to resist the toxic fandom exposed by the Gamergate controversy. Laying some groundwork for this resistance, the innovative romance gameplay in the *Mass Effect* series serves as a popular mechanic for LGBTQ and women players partly because it opposes the traditional gendering of romantic narratives as sentimental distractions. So-called hardcore action-adventure and SF gamers often demand that games maintain an exclusive, quasi-masochistic focus on manly physical and technological prowess disentangled from both romantic relationships as well as the Platonic intrusion of non-sexualized women into a testosterone-fueled boy's club. Such a patriarchal preference can be traced back in part to the foundational male insecurity in the formation of the SF genre and modern fan subcultures. Citing letters to the editor written by a young Isaac Asimov, Justine Larbalesteir, for instance, argues that romantic subplots in pulp-era space opera became a "contested site" (10) because these relationship-oriented narrative arcs were seen as emasculating to their audiences steeped in male-oriented wish-fulfillment. This began to change as feminist authors became more popular in the New Wave period of the SF genre, and, additionally, the SF women writers of the pulp era were recuperated by dedicated scholars. Joanna Russ, in her often-cited editorial "*Amor Vincit Foeminam*" (1980), hailed the power of feminist-utopian science fiction to reconfigure the feverish tropes and memes of "male supremacy" (13) that previously proliferated in the SF genre. Specifically, the editorial highlighted the vital need for a feminist-utopian movement to critically renovate the sexist trope of intergalactic encounters with all-female alien species whose civilizations were characterized by matriarchies, parthenogenesis, and lesbianism. Russ herself reworked this trope of a female-only society to startling effect in the portrayal of the unconventional women inhabitants of Whileaway in her own masterwork *The Female Man* (1975). *Mass Effect* aficionados will immediately recognize reimagined versions of the space-opera feminist-utopia genre material in the alien species known as the asari.

In 2007, Fox News presented a segment called "Se'Xbox? New Video Game Shows Full Digital Nudity and Sex", which censured *Mass Effect* as "Luke Skywalker meets *Debbie Does Dallas*" and fear-mongered about the corruption of children through what the network exaggeratedly deemed a pornographic sex scene featuring potential lesbian intimacy between FemShep and the asari character Liara T'Soni. Regardless of the carefully manufactured untruth of this non-scandal—the scene in question is tastefully discreet in its brief fleeting nudity—the segment does highlight the fact that sexual liaisons between aliens and humans continue to be a sensitive source of cultural anxiety in the popular SF imagination at large. Moreover, the uncannily humanoid asari directly tap into this cultural anxiety in their physical embodiment as biological difference. This estrangement is encoded as both strangely feminine and an unclassifiable, transgendered third sex; at one point, Liara tells Shepard, "male and female have no real meaning for us". Despite being genetically mono-gendered, the gender-fluid asari appear strikingly similar to humanoid women, except for their blue-colored skins and tentacle-like scalp crests. And in true feminist-utopian fashion, they engage in matriarchal social practices that suggest they consider themselves an all-female civilization, such as referring to kinship ties between members of their species as sisterhood and motherhood. Not unlike Octavia Butler's Oankali in her seminal *Xenogenesis* trilogy, the asari in *Mass Effect* are sex positive, cherishing and preserving the generation of life in all its infinite diversity, seeking to ensure their own reproductive survival, and pansexually hybridizing their gene pool with a wide range of alien species. The offspring of these unions all take on the primary physical characteristics of the asari, and so appear to the player to be blue-skinned tentacle-headed humanoid females. The asari call this process of parthenogenetic reproduction "embracing eternity".[4]

---

[4] See Chap. 5 for a discussion of the xenobiological evolutionary science behind the asari's parthenogenesis as a reproductive strategy.

In the first *Mass Effect*, when Lieutenant Commander Shepard first rescues Dr. Liara T'Soni during an attack by geth and a krogan battlemaster, she is helplessly floating in the air, trapped behind a security force field in an archeological dig on an uncharted world in the Artemis Tau cluster. The beautiful 106-year-young asari is at an early stage of her 1000-year-long life cycle that will progress from maiden, through matron, to matriarch. Maiden asari are broadly defined in psychological terms by their all-consuming curiosity, and while other asari court danger as professional mercenaries or search for self-expression as nightclub dancers, Liara has displaced such biological instincts to her archeological field research into the vanished alien civilization called the Protheans, of which she is one of the galaxy's leading experts. The player must initially decide whether to trust Liara since Shepard has been sent by Councilor Udina to investigate Liara's affiliation with her mother, Matriarch Benezia, who is in occult league with the villains of the game, namely, the rogue Specter Saren and the invading Reaper hoards. Perhaps intrigued by the prospect of Liara as a paramour, Shepard can choose to immediately release Liara from this security lock, but the chivalric sexism of this damsel-in-distress meet-cute is significantly short-circuited here in the FemShep playthrough. The queer romance between FemShep and Liara is unmistakably coded as lesbian, bisexual, and even transgendered, and hence the romantic subplot accrues new layers of cultural significance for its avid fandom. This narrative gameplay was exceptional for its time, and not only cemented BioWare's reputation as a vanguard purveyor of positive portrayals of LGBTQ identities in commercial videogames, but it also paved the way for progressive depictions of gender and sexuality in later high-profile and critically acclaimed games, such as in *The Last of Us* (2013) and *Life is Strange* (2015).

However, the queer characterization of Liara is also complicated and science-fictionally boundary-pushing, not easily reducible to an existing cultural stereotype. A great amount of fish-out-of-water humor throughout the first *Mass Effect* game derives from Liara being a bookish centenarian ingénue; the apt nickname Matriarch Benezia bestows on her fledgling child Liara is "Little Wing". More intricately developed than an amusing stock character, Liara completes a rounded, three-dimensional arc of character changes over the series in part because she is precariously poised on the cusp of her alien biological phase of matronhood. When a repentant but irreversibly corrupted Matriarch Benezia is killed by Shepard, Liara abandons some of her naiveté with the loss of a cherished female role model. Although the grieving Liara appreciates the paragon Shepard's gentle assessment that "the best of [her] mother lives on in [her]", namely Benezia's "strong, kind, and beautiful" life as an admirable asari matriarch before her indoctrination by Saren, Liara must nevertheless show resilience to overcome being unduly haunted by the dark, disturbingly complicit path that Benezia chose. Liara's parentage is further revealed in a more humorous way in *Mass Effect 3* when players learn that Liara's other mother, or nominal "father", the bartender Matriarch Aethyta, was the offspring of the hypermasculine species known as the krogan, making Liara a quarter krogan on a genetic level. Although Liara protests that the human understanding of gendered genetic inheritance does not apply to asari, she learns that this krogan background might make her prone to what Aethyta calls a testosterone-equivalent biochemical flood of "blood rage".

Feminist, queer, and allied gamers very much "ship" Liara/FemShep or "FemShiara", participating in the fan phenomenon of rooting for a romantic connection between characters, even when the explicit narrative only delicately suggests such a possible story development. When Liara uses her innate asari ability to meld minds with FemShep in order to decode the Prothean beacon message that has been stored in Shepard's mind, the FemShiara shipper will likely read this melding as romantically meaningful. Later, in conversation, Liara explains that the mystical fusion the asari refer to as a "union" is a much more intense and deeply romantic version of the mind meld that allows her to decode the message. The mind meld is a necessary narrative development of the overarching story of the game and can be interpreted as entirely platonic if the player chooses not to pursue a romance with Liara. After all, Liara's obsessive research has led her to suspect that the Protheans were only the latest phase in galaxy-wide, billion-year cycles of successive species extinctions; and as a remarkable specimen of close contact with the Prothean artifact, the intellectual puzzle of Shepard's experiences fascinates the scientifically minded Liara because the Prothean vision, if proven accurate, firmly establishes the legitimacy of her scholarly theories.

The romance gameplay options in *Mass Effect* allow otherwise implicit FemShiara shipping subtext to be turned into the overt text of a romantic subplot. If the player pushes to know more about her in private conversations, Liara will confess to embarrassment over expressing unprofessional interest in Shepard and to being intimidated by what seems like the frantic and bullying nature of the human species as compared to the glacial aging and tactful diplomacy of the asari. If the player continues to pursue conversations with Liara, she will explicitly declare a hesitant romantic interest. When FemShep asks whether the asari are open to lesbian or bisexual relationships, Liara insists that she is not gendered in the same way as humans, but then ambiguously tacks on, "perhaps we would fill what you consider a female role". In these conversations, Liara also hastens to dispel the crude myth that asari are promiscuous, thus inserting triangular competition over a rival into the romance arc of the game; hence if a bisexual FemShep has expressed romantic interest in the human male crewmember Kaiden Alenko, the conversational wheel will provoke politely jealous comments from both Kaiden and Liara until FemShep chooses to pursue a singular love interest.

In the romantic conversations that ensue, FemShep and Liara will express mutual astonishment over the opposites-attract magic of their companionate relationship. Liara will also marvel over what seems like either a great cosmic coincidence or the arcane workings of star-crossed destiny that enabled this trans-(alien) pairing. Such giddy conversational exchanges stress that the intermingling of the speculative space-opera trope of alien contact with the queer relationship reinforces the nonnormative dimension to this romantic subplot. As the romantic interludes arise between the overarching plots of the main missions, the gameplay also benefits from a tantalizing will-they/won't-they prolongation of a subtle conflict. For instance, Liara is at first overwhelmed by the chaotic emotions brought on by her relative inexperience. In gradual conversational developments, she expresses anxiety over whether FemShep understands her deep desire for a serious commitment and whether the grand endeavor of battling the Reapers threat should eclipse their otherwise inconsequential personal feelings. In these slowly unfolding conversational exchanges, some common relationship hazards may arise and FemShep can come off as too readily assuming the traditionally masculine roles associated with patriarchal attitudes toward women, such as the desire to be Liara's lord and protector, being brusquely uninterested in exclusive monogamy, or being too willing to sacrifice romance for the sake of official duty. However, the player can overcome these setbacks of dialogue-wheel options and move instead toward a meaningful and fulfilling relationship with Liara.

If the player has taken this path, FemShep and Liara can consummate their developing romance with a passionate sex scene at the end of the first *Mass Effect* game. Given the extreme lengthiness of the *Mass Effect* narrative saga, that game-climaxing union is only the beginning of FemShep and Liara's epic romance over the series, which resists the pernicious and widespread trope of "burying your gays", or depicting queer relationships as inevitably abortive and doomed. *Mass Effect 2* does begin with Liara being forced to witness FemShep's heroic sacrificial death as she attempts to save the remaining survivors when a Reaper-indoctrinated Collector ship destroys the Normandy in a surprise attack. However, prior to the main plotline of *Mass Effect 2*, Liara rescues Shepard's body from the Shadow Broker, a dreaded informational maven, saboteur, and profiteer in the cyber wars that spread sub rosa across the galaxy, and then Liara desperately gives Shepard to the humanity-first private-military contractor Cerberus in the hopes that they will be able to reanimate her into an undead cyborg.[5]

In the optional romantic subplot of *Mass Effect 2* and "The Lair of the Shadow Broker" extra downloadable content (DLC), Liara, who is still mourning the undead Shepard, seems hesitant to reignite an exclusive relationship with FemShep, especially as the beleaguered asari fends off a ruthless assassination attempt by an asari mercenary and seeks revenge for the kidnapping of her friend Feron, an ostensibly male member of the drell species, who has been taken hostage by her new nemesis, the Shadow Broker. In *Mass Effect 2*, Liara is substantially darker, grittier, more ethically compromised, and prone to cynicism than the untested post-adolescent ingénue introduced in the first *Mass Effect* game. From one particular queer and feminist perspective, it could be argued that this noirish, partly unsympathetic Liara has lost touch with the more cooperative and communal aspects of her asari values, becoming too readily complicit with the hypermasculine and heteronormative aggression, violence, and hostility that permeate the brutal colonial-capitalist politics of this galaxy. Understandably, then, a paragon FemShep is less romantically interested in this new ruthless edge to Liara's personality. The player can therefore choose the FemShep dialogue options that exhibit uncertainty over whether Shepard has lost her deep-seated respect for the woman she once loved. Once Shepard helps Liara supplant the Shadow Broker, though, FemShep and Liara's relationship can be rekindled, if so desired, but the

---

[5] These narrative events are discoverable through conversational exchanges in *Mass Effect 2*; however, in a well-orchestrated tie-in of transmedia synergy, they are not given direct recounting except in the comic-book series *Mass Effect: Redemption* written by BioWare lead writer Mac Walters and scripted by John Jackson Miller.

player will likely remain troubled and skeptical over whether FemShep can "keep honest" a woman who, arms spread grandiosely over an array of screens streaming secret data on all interstellar communications, gloats: "give me ten minutes and I can start a war". As discussed in Chap. 2, this book argues that a player might feel a shock of unseemly recognition when confronted with this new power-hungry and domineering development of the Liara character in *Mass Effect 2*, but they most likely will not unreservedly identify with this dark turn in the character's moral arc.

In its complex representation of the shifting gender-and-sexuality dynamics of Liara as a uniquely representative asari figure, the FemShiara romance of *Mass Effect 2* greatly benefits from a dissident resistance to clichéd tropes of maternity, nurturance, and caring all too unthinkingly linked to biologically essentialist notions of femininity. In *Mass Effect 3*, Liara proves instrumental to the primary plot of the series again, because she has uncovered a Prothean artifact, which contains the blueprint for a messianic doomsday device, the Crucible, and its activating component, the Catalyst. This colossal superweapon is the last-ditch hope all the sentient species have for warding off the imminent apocalyptic final phase of the Reaper invasion that is laying waste to the home worlds of every alien and human community in the galaxy. In this final game of the original series Liara is still the Shadow Broker, but she is also dramatically redeemed by her galaxy-saving commitment to stopping the Reapers. The FemShiara romance in *Mass Effect 3* is therefore less tragically conflicted than in *Mass Effect 2*, although some compelling jealousy-fueled complications do arise over the course of the game, such as the possibility of a lesbian love triangle with the human autistic savant Samantha Traynor. Liara and FemShep also grapple with FemShep's post-traumatic stress disorder from the terrifying Reaper invasion of Earth and Liara's regret and shame for not participating in the suicide mission to fight the collectors. When Shepard rescues Javik, the last surviving Prothean who had been cryogenically hibernating for 50,000 years, Liara is faced with more disturbing revelations about the Prothean civilization and its previously unknown technological bootstrapping of the asari culture.

Overall, though, if so chosen by the player, the FemShiara romance runs smoothly in *Mass Effect 3*, including in a touching conjugal scene in the captain's cabin, where Liara gifts FemShep the opportunity to script the entry of her own biography in an encyclopedic, virtually intelligent time capsule called a vigil that Liara constructs in case the Reapers win. In a reciprocating romantic gesture, FemShep can allow Liara to "write

[Shepard's] name in the stars", and the hagiographic entry that Liara dictates will be shaped by the idiosyncratic character customization the player has chosen throughout the series. Likewise, after a shore-leave sex scene in which the couple make bittersweet plans for the future beyond the impending extinction threat, Liara can gift Shepard her memories from the series in a mystic act of spiritual union prior to the climactic final battle of the series in which FemShep can sacrifice herself for her soul mate. The Liara character in *Mass Effect 3* is thus more melancholy but also more wisely mature and sympathetic in her large-hearted commitment to her paramour, thus substantially resolving the abrasive and vindictive aspects of her personality and the dubious complicity with the violent and aggressive patriarchy of the galactic power structures that complicated her character in the previous game. The critical feminist-utopian aspects of the asari culture also receive narrative reinforcement as Liara in the end embodies the love-conquers-all diplomatic savoir faire of a sophisticated species decidedly at odds, at least in idealistic principle, with the other more xenophobic, bellicose species of the galaxy. The *Mass Effect* series thereby provides cathartic closure to an extended, complex lesbian romance in a foregrounded narrative fashion that is exceptionally rare in popular media today.

Citing the rise of prominent female action heroes such as Lara Croft, recently rebooted in a significantly less objectified fashion in a prequel trilogy of *Tomb Raider* videogames (2013–2018), the folklorist Maria Tatar suggests that far from the "nice and narcotized" princess in the castle tower, the new "archetypal heroine" is depicted as "shooting 'em up, bobbing and weaving", straddling both stoic battlefield valor and being "caring and compassionate" (261). A writer for the *Mass Effect* series, Samantha Wallschlaeger likewise testifies to playing as FemShep inspired her to become a game writer since the character is "strong, smart, and brave … [and] no one treated her like she was somehow less than a man" (Qtd. in Marie 2018, 180). For, unlike the more problematic (but equally backlash-inducing) inclusion of women combatants in historical war games such as *Battlefield 5* (2018), the *Mass Effect* series does not subject its heroine to sexual harassment or gendered violence, leaping forward to a more egalitarian imagined future where such ritual degradations are no longer so regrettably omnipresent. Indeed, beyond the scope of the videogames themselves, FemShep has become a touchstone for the contemporary SF community, which regularly lauds the videogame universe for its representation of empowering women who embody "strength, loyalty, and tenacity" (Marie 2018, 97).

Another milestone of representation in the *Mass Effect* series can be found in the gay male romance between male Shepard and the human Lieutenant Steve Cortez, in the third installment of the series. This gay male romance option directly engages in what the SF scholar Wendy Gay Pearson has called "the overtly queer text" (19). Since the queerness of this character is embedded in such an extravagant futuristic space-opera setting, Steve Cortez's frank, empowered sexuality, although legitimated as unremarkable and commonplace in this universe, does not seem to be assimilated into the heteronormative standard of our own dominant historical culture. Rather, Cortez's competent, cyborg-like adeptness with unimaginably hyper-advanced technology evokes the utopian notion of collective queer futurity as a critical concept grounded in fluid, shifting notions of gender and sexuality.

The optional romantic subplot involving Steve Cortez also resists the stereotype of the promiscuous gay male. In contrast, Steve is a grieving widower whose husband, Robert, died during a Collector attack on Ferris Fields. Shepard can accidentally interrupt Steve weeping while listening compulsively to Robert's last recording before his death, a moving scene that indicates Steve's inability to emotionally move on. As options on the conversational wheel, the player as Shepard can choose to urge Steve to let go of his excessive grief. Shepard can then help with Steve's recovery from this trauma by encouraging him to visit the Memorial Wall for victims of Collector and Reaper attacks created in the refugee docks of the Citadel space station. This narrative choice has dire consequences, since if unchosen Steve will have become such an obsessive workaholic that his reaction times will be slowed, and he will die when his shuttle is shot down during the last Reaper assault on Earth. If the relationship is pursued following the Memorial Wall interaction, a male Shepard can then progress their romance beyond the friend stage while dancing with Steve at the Purgatory nightclub where they flirt, drink, and kiss. Steve's superior technological prowess is emphasized again when the pilot takes Shepard on a joy ride on the Kodiak shuttle and the two lovers experience the gravitational force of acceleration without inertial dampeners. Shepard and Steve declare their mutual commitment in this scene, which ends with Steve putting on the autopilot and the two cozily making out in the back of the shuttle. Far from stereotypical or tokenizing, the complexity of the emotional and physical connection between Steve and Shepard powerfully evokes the deep thematic concerns of the game, such as the existential balancing of the burdens of the past and urgency of the present, and the rekindling of passion by characters battered by loss, disappointment, and nostalgia.

As progressive as the inclusion of these queer romances was for a big-budget videogame of its era, savvy fans have been able to extend the game to embrace an even wider variety of racial and sexual identity options through customized "mods".[6] For instance, according to a BioWare animator, Jonathan Cooper, a same-sex romance option with the Black weapons-expert Jacob Taylor was cut from the final version of the game because "America was not ready" (Hart 2021). The *Mass Effect* modder, Ryan "Audemus" Ainsworth, has publicly voiced his viewpoint that such commercial diffidence in the face of racist and homophobic backlash is unfortunate: "I think the lack of LGBT representation in the *Mass Effect* trilogy is quite disappointing … especially since, for example, you can't get the full Paramour achievement in Legendary Edition if you play a strictly gay male Shepard" (Maher 2021). Remedying this oversight, on the popular website Nexus Mods, the modder Biganimefan2 created a "Same Sex Mod for Default Sheps" that restores same-sex romance options between male Shepard and Kaidan Alenko—a romance that the unmodified *Mass Effect 3* canonizes—or between FemShep and Ashley Williams. Moreover, YouTuber arik701 has modified a gay sex scene between Jacob Taylor and male Shepard by editing saved games. As of 2022, this popular video, "Mass Effect 2: Gay Romance with Jacob (Mod)", had been viewed over 240,000 times and accrued over 800 "likes".

The diverse popular appeal of the *Mass Effect* franchise has obviously struck a chord with a dynamic intersection of queer and feminist fandom and the SF literary community.[7] It is small wonder, then, that literary SF

---

[6] Modders have also added new ethnically identified hairstyles given the limited options in the official game. For instance, modders have created Afro-styled options, such as Afros and dreadlocks, for customized player avatars, which even in the latest official *Mass Effect: Legendary Edition* is only limited to fades and braids.

[7] While literary SF cannot hope to emulate the garden of forking paths available in a choice-driven role-playing game, all fictional narratives by definition necessitate a diverse proliferation of psychological fears, intentions, wishes, moral obligations, and haphazard knowledge of social circumstances gathered by characters, authors, and audiences, as influentially argued by Marie-Laure Ryan in the rigorous modal logic of possible worlds theory (Ryan 1991, 109–23). The infinite branching of pocket pseudo-realities is metaphysically embedded in fictional discourse, even in otherwise singular, linear, and unified narratives; therefore, the novelizations of *Mass Effect* might be said to highlight possible fictional story paths within the larger branching narrative structure of the explicitly more dynamic, nonlinear, and fictional videogame universe. The novelizations acknowledge this dynamic, unified nature of the *Mass Effect* story world by diligently avoiding mentioning in-universe events that could have variable outcomes or specifying the customizable traits of specific characters, especially the player avatar of Shepard, who are variously defined by the individual playthroughs of specific gamers.

allied with the inclusive representation of gender, sexuality, and race in SF culture would likewise seize on the rich depictions in *Mass Effect* of matriarchal succession, feminist utopia, and empowered sisterhoods to critically imagine alternative perspectives resistant to the dominant perspective of straight white male discourse. For instance, N.K. Jemisin, an enthusiastic fan of *Mass Effect*, after publishing the three-time consecutive Hugo-winning *Broken Earth* series of novels that significantly pushed boundaries for representations of race and gender in the SF genre, published the novelization *Mass Effect: Initiation* (2017), which she co-wrote with BioWare's creative director Mac Walters. The novelization takes place after the end of the original *Mass Effect* series but before the videogame narrative of *Mass Effect: Andromeda* begins, developing the backstory for the human Lieutenant Cora Harper, an NPC in the *Andromeda* videogame, who has powerful "biotics", or the biotechnologically enhanced capability to telekinetically incapacitate enemies. Trained by asari huntresses as part of the Valkyrie Program and joining the elite asari commando unit, Talein's Daughters, Cora develops intimate attachments with the feminist-utopian community of the asari during skirmishes on Omega and Nos Astra colonies fending off geth invaders. Nevertheless, interestingly developing the problematic of xenophobia that suffuses the *Mass Effect* universe, Jemisin and Walters write Cora such that she suffers intensely from imposter syndrome, as the sole human in an elite asari commando unit who she understandably feels are physically and mentally superior to humans. Enamored by the empowered abilities of the asari, Cora also struggles with the anxiety of seeking matriarchal approval and affirmation from her imperious asari mentor Nisira. Through the internalized prejudice of Cora's feelings of not deserving inclusion in the idealized alien sisterhood and matriarchy of the asari commandos, the novel complexly explores political issues of marginality and privilege, belonging and invisibility, that equally pervade conversations about gender, sexuality, and race.

In her self-imposed adoration of and exclusion from the alien utopian matriarchy and sisterhood, Cora nurtures a sublime, anxious fascination with the prospect of an alien all-female solidarity as radically estranged from the chauvinistic status quo of our standard human perspective today. This anxiety recurs in the action-packed plot when Cora is first betrayed by asari commando sister Ygara Menoris and later when she is induced by means of a cognitive implant into a Krogan blood rage to combat genetically modified human-derived monstrosities modified by a rogue AI. In these incidents, perhaps as much as a particularly feminist playthrough of

FemShep in the original *Mass Effect* series might also perform, Cora negotiates her torn loyalties as an asari-aligned but all-too-human woman warrior who balances both courage and compassion, an aggressive protector of an alien feminist utopia, and a poised peace-maker capable of self-confidence and caring. In the heat of battle, Cora remembers a parable of a heroic asari matriarch that parallels Cora's own hard-won epiphany at the end of the novel; before launching into a hail of enemy fire, the matriarch dismisses the idea that she should survive the war to care for and nurture her daughters back on Thessia by declaring *"I have only one lesson to teach them. The most important lesson that any mother can teach her children—to fight!"* (227, emphasis in original). By battling her deep-seated sense of inadequacy and self-loathing as much as the rampaging menace of hyper-masculine, genetically modified cyborgs, by the end of the novel, Cora has finally fully absorbed this lesson—a fiercely maternal piece of instruction that is pointedly not biologically inborn but learned through inculcated experience—a lesson in gendered resilience, inclusion, and resistance.

Challenging an essentialist or stereotypical account of gender distinctions, the literary novelizations of *Mass Effect* underscore the wide variety of viewpoints representable by alien female characters in the videogames. Hence the Hugo, Otherwise, and Locus award-winner Catherynne M. Valente wrote *Mass Effect: Annihilation* (2018) as another sequel to the original *Mass Effect* trilogy and prequel to *Mass Effect: Andromeda* that extends the characterization of alien gender and sexuality developed in the videogames. Valente's space-operatic locked-room mystery is populated by an all-alien contingent of the quarian ark ship *Keelah Si'Yah* that is delayed on its faster-than-light 600-year trip from the Milky Way to the Andromeda galaxy when its cryogenic bays are sabotaged by a manufactured pathogen dubbed the Fortinbras variant by a *Hamlet*-obsessed elcor. As if carefully decentering the BroShep perspective in a *Mass Effect* videogame playthrough, Valente's book follows four interesting alien women "sleepwalkers" assigned to investigate the deaths of hundreds of drell, while the rest of the tens of thousands of alien passengers remain cryogenically asleep. The detection of a noirish mystery by a female detective emulates some hard-boiled episodes that a player might run though as a FemShep avatar, especially the Liara-centric "Lair of the Shadow Broker" DLC.

In Valente's *Mass Effect: Annihilation*, the female members of the sleepwalker team include the drell systems analyst Anax Therion, the volus engineer Irit Non, the batarian crime queen Borbala Ferank, and the quarian technology specialist and team leader, Senna'Nir vas Keelah Si'Yah.

The intricately developed characterization of these various alien women is epitomized by Anax Therion, a chameleonic assassin spy for the Shadow Broker. No passive or helpless observer, Anax expertly elicits intimate information from companions by modifying her backstory as well as her "micro-gestures, vocal tone, dialect, personal anecdotes, each of them infinitely variable to the needs of the millisecond" (98). As a drell, the reptilian Anax is also both blessed and cursed by involuntary seizures of eidetic memory, which Anax also deftly exploits to craft her own life history to be more vivid and compelling to her interlocuters, all of whom she suspiciously investigates like a master gumshoe. In no way diminished or weakened by these biological markers of alien difference, Anax deepens our understanding of the gender dynamics of the drell species, since the original videogame series of *Mass Effect* only represents male versions of this species. Much like the asari commandos resist prejudicial notions of feminine otherness in their depiction as fierce but diplomatic warriors evocative of sublime wonder and awe in Jemisin's novelization, so the female drell Anax exercises an astoundingly preternatural competence as a master of disguise, observation, and induction, cognitive-epistemological skills primed for the solving of puzzling crimes.

In an ingenious twist on the customizable narrative branching of the videogame series, Valente's novelization also creates multiple, inconsistent backstories for Anax, suggesting perhaps that the essential femaleness of the drell amounts to a nebulous, even arbitrary social construct. Anax quickly intuits that the volus fashion designer Irit Non has "resentment toward males" (150) because her father is the notorious Gaffno Yap, an anarcho-socialist agitator and traitor to the hyper-capitalist, commerce-worshiping volus species. Therefore, while being suited in a volus suit to quarantine her from the Fortinbras viral infection "her arms held out to the side like an aristocrat's wife being fitted for a ballgown", (149) Anax weaves a self-mythologizing story of cross-species solidarity of the feminist proletariat about being sold to Oleon, a member of the floating jellyfish alien species called the hanar, by an unscrupulous tyrannical father figure of a drell disappointed in her feminine failings. While not provably false, this oversimplifying self-narrative conflicts with the stories she tells the criminal mastermind batarian Borbala Ferank about being adopted by a conniving Oleon, with whom she enters into a state of indentured servitude called the Compact, and the story she tells the quarian Malak'Rafa, who has fallen in love with his platonic friend, the female captain of the ark ship. Anax suggests to Malak'Rafa that she had illicit, unconsummated trans(-alien) love

for Oleon, who bought her from a cruel master who was a zealous prosely-
tizer for a religious cult. Interestingly, all these various contradictory narratives turn on the complicated megahistory from the videogame series and
the world-building details that the hanar rescued hundreds of thousands of
drell from extinction on their desert home world and transported them to
the ocean world Kahje, thus creating the historical Compact, or debt of
gratitude in which the intensely spiritual drell serve their species by fulfilling tasks requested by hanar. Even though the hanar are technically gen-
derless, the enforced hierarchy implicit in the enacting of this historical
Compact echoes patriarchal power structures dominant in gendered discourse, and Anax powerfully manipulates this anti-patriarchal discourse
among these empowered women to assist her investigation.

Systemic exclusion from masculinized positions of privilege and entitlement, and the fostering of sectarian cultures of resentment and retaliation
among the oppressed that such exclusion logically engenders, drives the
solving of the mystery. Anax's last partially true backstory preys on
Malak'Rafa's xenophobic fears of interspecies Compacts and proves especially useful for solving the mystery, since it is revealed that the ark ship
captain is responsible for the Fortinbras virus due to the quarian's vengeful
desire to oust the prominence of the Council species in the Andromeda
galaxy by depopulating their numbers on the ark. Leading to unintended
collateral damage, this plot backfires when the equally subordinated
drell—whose immune systems are weakened by a congenital disease called
Kepral's Syndrome, due to the aforementioned transportation to the
hanar water world—are the first to die from an unexpected mutant strain
of the pathogen. The xenophobic mass murderer ark ship captain can
therefore be seen as a complicated foil that perversely extends Anax's
fraught identification with her own vulnerable minority community, since
it is out of species loyalty that Anax endeavors to discover the killers of her
drell shipmates. When Borbala Ferank, a member of the batarian species
notorious for being slavers, mercenaries, and warlords, earlier admits to
being a painter after Anax asks her not to shoot her in the back, Anax
reproaches herself for her willingness to indulge in easy, divisive stereotypes, "batarians were criminals, drell died young. It was all in a good
day's space prejudice" (103). Before Anax finally re-enters cryogenic sleep
at the end of the novel, she first reveals to Borbala that she was never
bonded to a hanar at all but was sadly overlooked for the honorable performance of such a Compact. Regardless of whether this story is another
clever fabrication, by confessing this partial (un)truth unprovoked, which

non-coincidentally defies space prejudices about her species, and agreeing to meet up with Borbala in Andromeda, Anax undermines and contests her own previously nurtured xenophobic bias about the impossibility of multi-species camaraderie and feminist solidarity, which, ultimately, derives from the aggressive interstellar politics of distrust, marginalization, and prejudice that set the grisly mystery in motion to begin with.

This chapter has argued that the introduction of a playable female avatar in BioWare's *Mass Effect* series helped to usher in more inclusive and equitable attitudes toward diverse representations of women in the male-dominated videogame industry. The elaborate narratives that feature admirable and compelling ethnic minorities either as the customizable playable character or as a significant non-playable character are likewise laudable and important contributions to videogame and popular culture at large. Moreover, the videogame series, as well as the modding culture it spawned, should be recognized as a landmark in its bold challenging of the homophobic, racist, and misogynist backlash that has become especially virulent online in recent years. The depictions of gay, lesbian, and non-binary romances in the *Mass Effect* series are especially noteworthy for their nuance and complexity in the annals of contemporary popular culture. That this inclusive, pluralist attitude has begun to seep into a broader culture beyond the videogame audience can be glimpsed in the literary novelizations that similarly inject discourses of gender, race, and sexuality into the widescreen-baroque space-opera setting of the videogames.

References

BioWare. 2007. *Mass Effect 1*. BioWare. PC/Mac/Consoles.
———. 2010. *Mass Effect 2*. BioWare. PC/Mac/Consoles.
———. 2012. *Mass Effect 3*. BioWare. PC/Mac/Consoles.
———. 2021. *Mass Effect: Legendary Edition*. BioWare. PC/Mac/Consoles.
deWinter, Jennifer, and Carly A. Kocurek. 2017. "Aw Fuck, I Got a Bitch on my Team!": Women and the Exclusionary Cultures of the Computer Game Complex. In *Gaming Representation: Race, Gender, and Sexuality in Video Games*, ed. Jennifer Malkowski and Treaandrea M. Russworm, 57–74. Bloomington: Indiana University Press.
Guisao, Jason. 2022. Celebrating Respectful Representations of Blackness in Gaming. *Game Informer*, February 14. https://www.gameinformer.com/2022/02/14/celebrating-respectful-representations-of-blackness-in-gaming
Hart, Aimee. 2021. Jacob from *Mass Effect* Gay Romance Was Cut Because "America Wasn't Ready for It." *Gayming Magazine*, January 28. https://gaymingmag.com/2021/01/jacob-from-mass-effect-gay-romance

Jemisin, N.K., and Mac Walters. 2017. *Mass Effect: Initiation*. London: Titan Books.

Kane, Matt. 2011. *Dragon Age 2* Writer Defends Game's Commitment to LGBT Inclusivity. *Glaad.org*, March 28. https://www.glaad.org/2011/03/28/dragon-age-2-writer-defends-games-commitment-to-lgbt-inclusivity.

Kaplan, Cora. 1993. Dirty Harriet/Blue Steel: Feminist Theory Goes to Hollywood. *Discourse* 15 (1): 50–70.

Larbalestier, Justine. 2002. *The Battle of the Sexes in Science Fiction*. Middletown: Wesleyan University Press.

Livi, Aubrey. 2017. A Brief History of BioWare's LGBTQ Inclusion. *Brinkbit*, 5 July. https://medium.com/brinkbit/a-brief-history-of-biowares-lgbtq-inclusion.

Maher, Cian. 2021. *Mass Effect* Legendary Edition Has Sparked a "Modding Renaissance". *The Gamer*, 22 June. https://www.thegamer.com/mass-effect-legendary-edition-modding-renaissance.

Marie, Meagan. 2018. *Women in Gaming: 100 Professionals of Play*. Indianapolis: Penguin.

Pearson, Wendy Gay. 1999. Alien Cryptographies: The View from Queer. *Science Fiction Studies* 26 (1): 1–22.

Phillips, Amanda. 2020. Does Anyone Really Identify with FemShep? Troubling Identity (and) Politics in Mass Effect. In *Gamer Trouble: Feminist Confrontations in Digital Culture*. New York: New York University Press.

Russ, Joanna. 1980. *Amor Vincit Foeminam*: The Battle of the Sexes in SF. *Science-Fiction Studies* 7 (1): 2–15.

Ryan, Marie-Laure. 1991. *Possible Worlds, Artificial Intelligence, and Narrative Theory*. Bloomington: Indiana University Press.

Sarkeesian, Anita. 2016. Body Language and the Male Gaze. *Feminist Frequency*, March 31. https://feministfrequency.com/video/body-language-the-male-gaze/

Sohovnen, Tanja. 2020. Game Characters as Tools of Expression: Modding the Body in Mass Effect. In *Women and Videogame Modding: Essays on Gender and Digital Community*, ed. Bridget Whelan. Jefferson: McFarland.

Tatar, Maria. 2021. *The Heroine with 1001 Faces*. New York: W.W. Norton & Company.

Urquhart, Evan. 2021. I Insist You Play *Mass Effect* as a Woman. *Slate*, May 18. https://slate.com/culture/2021/05/mass-effect-legendary-edition-ps4-xbox-pc-femshep.html

Valente, Catherynne M. 2018. *Mass Effect: Annihilation*. London: Titan Books.

Voorhees, Gerald. 2012. Neo-liberal Multiculturalism in Mass Effect: The Government of Difference in Digital RPGs. In *Dungeons, Dragons, and Digital Denizens*, ed. Gerald Voorhees, Joshua Call, and Katie Whitlock, 259–277. New York: Continuum International Publishing Group.

CHAPTER 5

"Science Fun Today": *Mass Effect* and Rethinking SF's Pedagogical Approach to Exoplanetary and Astrobiological Science

In the first *Mass Effect*, perhaps while pursuing a promising lead on Saren's secret base on the planet Virmire in the Hoc star system, a player may choose to survey nearby planets to scout for useful Alliance mineral resources. One such planet is named Jarfor, and its description screen when pulled up by the player reads the following: "Jarfor is a close-orbiting 'hot Jupiter' hydrogen-helium gas giant … in composition it is extraordinarily similar to 51 Pegasi's planet Bellerophon (one of the first extrasolar planets discovered by humanity in the late 20th century)". In a clever future-historical allusion, *Mass Effect* thereby highlights one of the signal breakthroughs of contemporary real-world astronomy, namely, the advent of the rapidly developing field of extrasolar planetary science. Indeed, the first extrasolar planet, or exoplanet, discovered, in 1995, by future Nobel Laureates Michel Mayor and Didier Queloz, was 51 Pegasus B, a so-called hot Jupiter, since its immense size and gaseous composition initially puzzled astronomers whose theories of solar-system formation excluded the creation of cold gas Jupiter-sized planets close to their suns. Not only did the discovery of 51 Pegasus B spearhead a new spectroscopic toolkit available to contemporary astronomy—pioneering the so-called radial velocity technique that measures the doppler effect of tiny gravitational wobbles in a star pulled by an orbiting planet—it also ushered in a groundbreaking new theory of solar-system formation in which gas giants could migrate inward due to the complex orbital mechanics of planetary disks.

© The Author(s), under exclusive license to Springer Nature Switzerland AG 2023
J. Winter, *BioWare's Mass Effect*, Palgrave Science Fiction and Fantasy: A New Canon,
https://doi.org/10.1007/978-3-031-18876-3_5

In the videogame, rather than being a token Easter egg, though, the surveying of exoplanets represents a key science-educational feature that is deeply integrated into the full panoply of game mechanics and story worlds available to the scientifically curious player in the *Mass Effect* series. As they continue to peruse the description of Jarfor, for instance, the interested players may be piqued by the following astounding fact: "the temperature difference between the sunward 'hot pole' and the dark side 'cold pole' creates constant hurricane force winds". This statement indeed accords with the astronomically credible idea that the magnified solar heat of orbiting so close to its sun could likely drive winds on a planet like 51 Pegasi B to blow at thousands of miles per hour. Later in the game series, when scanning planets in *Mass Effect 2*, this knowledge about the sweltering effect of the orbital radius on a hot Jupiter may be recalled when scanning and mining the planet Volturno, in the Aquila System. It is important to note here that players will likely happily perform these Zen-like tasks of the space-simulation, or "space-sim", mini-game since scanning and mining planets in *Mass Effect 2* orchestrates a broad, interconnected system of narrative goals and game mechanics. The palladium, platinum, and iridium mined from Volturno, for instance, can be saved to sell to merchants for credits useful in equipping characters for combat or to research upgrades for the Normandy starship, whose outfitting of weapons, shields, and armor will help in turn determine how suicidal the suicide mission at the game's finale turns out to be.

In addition to stacking up one's mineral resources, a dawning scientific understanding of some of the plausible astronomical underpinnings of this seemingly far-fetched space-opera universe also promises to increase, as the observant player reads that Volturno is a "super Earth". On this screen, the player can also simultaneously view various planetological data—such as orbital distance, Keplerian ratio, atmospheric pressure, mass, and so on—and note that the radius of this planet is 11,177 kilometers, or nearly twice the size of Earth, and its surface gravity is 3.3 times that of Earth. This data turns out to be more or less plausible extrapolation on the real astronomical phenomenon of a super Earth. As in the case of hot Jupiters, the actually observed astronomical phenomena of super Earths contradict said planetesimal theoretical paradigms about solar-system formation but turn out upon recent empirical discoveries to be surprisingly common, relatively speaking. For instance, in a much-publicized series of highly debated discoveries, between 2005 and 2010, the relatively dim red dwarf star Gliese 581 was found to possibly contain upward to four super Earths in its close orbit, and in the equally sensational case of Kepler-11, in 2011, a star in the Cygnus constellation was shown to contain a staggering five super Earths within a Mercury-sized orbit.

If the science-minded player of *Mass Effect* were then to research super Earths outside of the game, they would soon realize that the phenomenon is a lightning rod of contemporary astronomical research. As explained by the astrophysicist Elizabeth Tasker, for instance, the investigation into super Earths presents astronomy today with severe challenges to core scientific paradigms that assume our own solar system is normal. Moreover, the study of super Earths expands the frontiers of astronomy by presenting fundamentally uncertain dilemmas about star-system formation, such as whether the gravitational force of hot Jupiters acts as a cosmic broom that assists in the development of super Earths, or whether a magnetic dead zone from the star interacts with a planetary gas headwind to create the massive planets (Tasker 2017, 105–110). Even if the pursuit of this tantalizing thread of non-required, extra-game research is handily declined by the player, the planet-scanning of Jarfor and Volturno confronts even the most casual players of the *Mass Effect* series with seemingly bizarre star systems radically different from our own. Despite the defamiliarizing effect of this game dynamic, the dense exoplanetary world-building of the videogame series also nevertheless invokes a cognitive cachet of plausible astronomical "hardness". This hypnotic mystique of well-researched scientific credibility and verisimilitude couches the otherwise fantastic world-building in a realistic attention to concrete detail.

The gameplay dynamic in *Mass Effect* owes many of its broadest contours to the popular subgenre of space-sim videogames, and specifically, the prototypical exemplar of *Elite* (1984), and its randomly generated star systems three-dimensionally navigable by player-controlled spacecraft, followed up by its more astonishingly astronomically accurate sequel *Elite Dangerous* (2014). Designed by David Braben and programmed by Ian Bell, *Elite* set the template for the space sim and its "exploration of a large universe within which many activities are possible, from trading and mining to piracy and bounty hunting" (Tringham 2015, 414). Likewise, in terms of the literary and cultural history of space opera as a subgenre, interweaving rhapsodies of plausible scientific exposition, speculation, and ingenuity into story-driven fictional narratives is foundational to what Gary Westfahl calls the "pedagogical model" (40) for hard SF that traces back at least to Hugo Gernsback's influential editorials for the pulp magazine *Amazing Stories*.

Given BioWare's history of being founded by medical doctors, and its early role in producing medical diagnostic games, it seems appropriate that one of the creators of the *Mass Effect* series, Casey Hudson, who holds a degree in mechanical engineering, views the space-opera conventions of the videogame as immensely entertaining scaffolding that could make astronomy and biology tangible and meaningful to the average gamer. In an interview with NASA educator Sara Mitchell, Hudson explains the genesis of the intense focus on plausible science in the videogame: "the underlying idea was that real-life scientific discoveries consistently create imagery and concepts that blow away previous notions of what is possible". This nuanced idea that implies the paradigm-shifting science in *Mass Effect* partakes in equal parts cognition and estrangement also aligns with the pedagogical approach that many working scientists echo when they testify to their youthful enthusiasm for the SF genre. In an article for *Scientific American,* for instance, astrophysicist Sean Carroll champions *Mass Effect* for its modest but instrumental contribution to science education, speculating that "someone might hear [a scientific term] as part of a game and then hear it again in a more scientific context, and that might help them ultimately gain a better understanding of what it is" (Greenemeier 2010).

Moreover, this chapter argues that treatment of science in *Mass Effect* injects into the pedagogical model of traditional space-opera cutting-edge, doubt-laden uncertainties that subvert a clumsy science-to-public "transmission model" of science education, outreach, and communication. Such a monolithic model presumes the need for rarefied expertise to correct the stubborn passivity, confusion, and ignorance of the general audience. Hence the explanatory references to super Earths and hot Jupiters in the space-sim feature of the *Mass Effect* series do not simply inform the benighted gamer but rather such speculation acclimates the gamer to the rigor of contemporary scientific debates that swirl around exoplanetary phenomena. The educationally engaged gamer helps to construct, transform, and even democratize a speculative and contestatory approach to the science depicted since videogame narratives, as Janet Murray has influentially argued, emphasize that Coleridge's famous idea of an immersive "suspension of disbelief" is all too passive of a formulation to apply to the narrative agency that the videogame medium encourages (Murray 1997, 110). In other words, *Mass Effect* does not force-feed rote scientific trivia on otherwise clueless, inert gamers. Instead, the game elicits a fun, participatory ethos toward the active, ongoing construction of scientific knowledge that makes stakeholders mindful of the stakes bound up with living in a science-saturated society.

A telling example of this critical, speculative approach to otherwise impressively hard and plausible astronomy is the mineral resource known as Element Zero, a major SF "novum" in *Mass Effect*. A novum is an extrapolative future discovery or invention that radiates out expanding ripples of narrative consequences and influence. As per the Codex, Element Zero, or Eezo for short, is an exotic material responsible for the faster-than-light space travel of the mass-effect relays and for the superpowers known as "biotic" singularities that specially customized players can wield with swirling blue panache in combat. More than this efficient and immersive narrative scaffolding, though, the videogame posits—as a wary player who heeds the travel advisory to the planet Haestrom may discover—that Element Zero can be artificially cultivated from the remnants of a "neutron star" emitting so-called dark energy. A quarian colony seems to have investigated Haestrom's neutron star before being overrun by the rogue artificially intelligent geth. The parent star Dholen was about to unexpectedly balloon into a red giant and its transformation seems to be inexplicably bound up with these unusual dark-energy emissions.

Outside its archly exaggerated fictional incorporation into the game, Element Zero is indeed an unverified, theoretical atom consisting of neutrons with no protons or electrons; it was first proposed by the chemist Andreas von Antropoff, in 1926, who placed it at the beginning of the periodic table elements. Later chemists codified and renamed Element Zero in scientific literature as "neutronium", or, more commonly now, neutron-degenerate matter. As Sean Carroll explains, scientists also hypothesize that a neutron star, or an extremely dense ball of energy that is created when a supermassive star implodes, could indeed be somehow bound up with the mysterious matter they reluctantly label dark energy, an elusive and frequently theorized phenomenon that may mathematically explain the acceleration of the universe (Carroll 2007, 53). Dark energy is theorized to strangely escape the event horizon of black holes, which, according to Stephen Hawking's seminal ideas, may in fact become micro-sized.

This improbable speculation about dark energy contributing to biotic superpowers and faster-than-light travel is, of course, a soaring fantasy. Yet hard, if abstruse science does indeed firmly underpin the improbable foray of the *Mass Effect* series into the uncanny realm of dark energy, neutron stars, and black holes. While some detractors might contend that the

cognitive leaps of biotics and mass effects are tantamount to at best popu-
larized distortion of science and at worst crackpot pseudoscience, such
leaps are not arbitrary distractions but rather essential to the compelling
space-opera narrative and the interactive combat gameplay. As Colin
Milburn in *Mondo Nano* argues in terms of the proliferating science-
steeped references to nanotechnology that similarly pervade both science
fiction and videogames, the attraction for such specialized frontiers of scientific research for the precise pleasure that SF gamers seek lies in the
buoyant air of unsolved mystery and a participatory openness to vigorous
debates over such issues in both the scientific community and the public at
large. Contending that the scientific content found in videogames has
both referential and speculative dimensions, Milburn convincingly writes
that the chosen preoccupations of science itself are likewise shaped by such
popular discourse: "the constant slippage between simile and metonymy
reveals the extent to which such concepts orient scientific discourse toward
particular visions of the future" (40).[1]

   Some of the most visually striking as well as astronomically accurate
instances of imagery in the casual space-sim mini-game aspects of *Mass
Effect* are the interstellar nebula, which are the particolored, fluorescent
clouds of gauzy material that the player, after commanding Shepard to
zoom in on the holographic galaxy map on the bridge, navigates the
Normandy through to travel to specific star systems. After zooming in
from an overview of the Milky Way galaxy map from which galactic arms
and clusters are visible, and before zooming in on interplanetary-scale
solar systems, the nebula graphics screens derive from famous artistic ren-
derings of nebular cosmic phenomena, colorized to display infrared,

---

[1] The fan-generated online website *Mass Effect Wiki* reproduces the data about these planets from the space-sim portion of the game. It also testifies to the ways in which the *Mass
Effect* fanbase champions a dynamic slippage between scientific cognition and speculative
estrangement in the game, much in line with Hal Clement's influential observation about the
nature of scientific world-building in the SF genre. Offered in an essay entitled "Whirligig
World" that served as an introduction to later editions of his prototypical hard SF novel
Mission to Gravity (1954), Clement claims hard SF can be distinguished by the avidity of its
readers who are always on the lookout for factual slipups or cheating in the genre contract of
scientific verisimilitude as part of their fundamental reading experience. Likewise, perhaps no
better evidence of the hard SF credentials of *Mass Effect* can be found than in the errata that
accompanies the *Mass Effect Wiki*, such as the note to the planet Antida that cites an astronomy textbook and notes that, according to the provided data about the radius and orbital
period, the world is much too small to be classified as a standard hydrogen-helium gas giant,
and the planet should be relabeled as a superterrestrial protoplanet.

ultraviolet, gamma, and X-ray signals, and originally photographed by astoundingly powerful telescopes, such as the Hubble Space Telescope. Some of the names assigned to the nebula likewise more or less correspond to their scientifically familiar celestially cartography, including the Snake Nebula, the Horsehead Nebula, the Eagle Nebula, the Crescent Nebula, and the Omega Nebula.

Hence it is not surprising that in the previously mentioned interview with Casey Hudson, Sara Mitchell reports a NASA-insider response to the game: "the first time I caught a glimpse of the astronomical imagery in the *Mass Effect* videogames, I was blown away by how realistic everything looked". Yet it is also important to remember that each one of these nebulae serve as cosmic staging grounds for vital missions in the overarching narrative of the game series; hence, as Hudson hastens to add in the interview, sharing credit with a variety of science consultants and the diverse teams of science-informed writers who contributed to the game, the remarkable verisimilitude of *Mass Effect* is not merely gratuitous window-dressing. Hudson states, "you don't need to understand all the science to appreciate the story" but notes the narrative "feels like it makes sense" because the game sets "intimate emotions against an epic and believable science-fiction backdrop". In other words, the means by which the seemingly arcane science is made meaningful to players is the implicit analogy between the aesthetically pleasing graphics—that is, the rainbow-colored kaleidoscope of nebular oceans the Normandy pilots around—and the teeming plurality of extraterrestrial intelligence that permeates the space opera. After all, by fantastic leaps of the popular imagination, the spectroscopic analyses of nebula have long been coupled with sublime fascination and terror over the search for life in the universe.[2]

[2] See, for example, Robert Markley who contends that from Pierre-Simon Laplace and William Herschel's eighteenth-century theories, through Percival Lowell's Victorian claims that there were canals on Mars, through NASA's flyby telescopes, satellites, probes, and landers in the late twentieth century, and continuing to the wide-ranging multiplicity of global and commercial missions of space exploration today, the evolving nebular hypothesis, which now is very distinct from the planetesimal hypothesis from which it derives, has been historically bound up with "promoting the role of speculation in planetary science and suggesting strategies to uncover or rule out life on Mars" (243). Indeed, in a knowing nod to the outsized role the red planet has played in planetary science, the codex of *Mass Effect* informs the player that the first discovered Prothean artifact that instigates this space opera was discovered on Mars. And in a mesmerizing mission in *Mass Effect 3*, the player controls Shepard as they attempt to rescue Liara, who is busy excavating a key to defeating the Reaper invasions, from a Cerberus attack during a storm on the surface of Mars.

In exoplanetary science, the hectic search for the Earthlike planets in the so-called Goldilocks or habitable zone of a solar system is a primary avenue through which science is negotiated with the public. This rhetorical framework may at first blush seem bizarre since relatively small Earthlike planets are not easily detectable by the spectroscopic tools handy to the planet hunter, including the radial velocity technique, the transit method, direct imaging, or gravitational lensing. Nevertheless, for popular dissemination, the data-rich and empirically rigorous scientific inquiry into the material nature of the universe requires a focal point of an adventurous quest for the vanishingly tiny speck of observable "biosignatures" in the cosmic immensities. Pointedly eschewing the label "Earthlike", *Mass Effect* instead identifies the habitable planets "garden worlds", and the series so far has racked up a robust seventy-nine of them. The utter strangeness of many of these garden worlds, however, severely tests the anthropocentric bias at the intersection of exoplanetary science and the search for extraterrestrial life. When surveying and mining planets, the exploratory player encounters not only lush tropical paradises (Virmire), and not just hot Jupiters and super Earths but also lava planets (Therum), ice worlds (Hyetiana), water planets with nitrogen atmospheres (Yamm), high-gravity worlds (Dekuuna), worlds with weak magnetic fields and high solar radiation (Palaven), worlds with liquid ammonia oceans (Patavig), and borderline garden worlds with lethal allergens (Nordacrux) and toxic-hazard microbes (Eletania).[3]

Moreover, the exotic life forms that spawn from these exoplanetary garden worlds in *Mass Effect* both disrupt and reinforce the anthropocentric bias that also limits astrobiology, the modern speculative science that studies what extraterrestrial life in the universe might possibly look like. In the service of overturning a reductive transmission model of science education, the videogame series escapes the charge of presuming biology determines destiny. The diverse proliferations of alien species explode an overly narrow understanding of scientific principles and the seemingly infinite richness and variety of biological phenomena. For instance, as

---

[3] There are also many interesting non-habitable worlds in *Mass Effect* available to survey and even sometimes make planetfall and explore in either a vehicle (the Mako) or spacesuits, including ice dwarfs with highly elliptical orbits (Tenoth), rogue planets without solar systems (H523), extrasolar captures (Cyllene), mini-Neptunes (Huiton), protoplanetary chondrite meteorites (Beyalt), planets with ancient remnants of "Jupiter brains", that is, planet-sized supercomputer megastructures (Phoba), and in campy homage to the classic SF film *Forbidden Planet* (1956), worlds that host "monsters from the Id" (Junthor).

gradually revealed through the lore of the series, the overarching cosmic clash between sentients and organics might be said to revolve around the competitive exclusion principle, or the partitioning of ecological niches with a scarcity of resources that necessitates over epic time scales an evolutionary arms race between the trophic levels of predators, parasites, and prey.

The last living member of the Prothean species, Javick, explains that the competitive exclusion principle, and the biological struggle to survive and propagate, is a baseline amoral reality in the natural world, to Shepard, with his characteristic brutal bluntness: "Stand amongst the ashes of a trillion dead souls and ask the ghosts if honor matters". Javick would know whereof he speaks, of course, since the Protheans, a species with exceptional reproductive success across the galaxy, were wiped out and parasitized (what the Reapers call "ascending") by the rise of a more powerful competitor. This existential threat turns out to be a vast experiment in artificial intelligence gone wrong, an attempt by self-aware machines, the Reapers, to harvest sufficiently advanced species potential over cycles of eons. At the end of *Mass Effect* 3, it is revealed that the Catalyst, the central processing unit of the Reapers, concocts the perverse final solution of the harvest for ostensibly Darwinian purposes. Based on their original programming protocol and algorithmically testing out alternatives over unfathomable immensities of time and space, the Reapers hope to optimize self-preservation for all biological life across the longest conceivable timelines. According to the Catalyst, this prospect eternally fails given that the competitive exclusion principle can induce extinctions, not to mention the inevitable civilizational downward spirals of mutually assured destruction that organic life is heir to. *Mass Effect* derives some of its most sublime moments of scientific horror in the series from narrative climaxes that imply the apparent intricate design of evolution is in fact purposeless, redundant, and undirected, not divinely teleological but brutally crude and random, hurtling toward endless cycles of chaos.

Lest the player assume game tacitly endorses the brutal Darwinian logic of the Reaper's periodic harvests, though, it should be remembered that they are the melodramatic villains of the series. The game also links the development of its protagonist alien species to other biological imperatives often opposed to the competitive exclusion principle: namely, for instance, the adaptive fitness inherent in altruistic behavior, co-evolution, and kin selection. In particular, despite their clandestine intrigues, the long-lived asari treasure cooperation, reciprocity, and alliance-building to the point of discrete individuals essentially participating in an emergent psychic hive mind of species being. Real-world analogies that xenobiologists draw on to explicate the evolutionary advantages of biological cooperation can be found in phenomena as varied as termite nests, ant hills, rabbit warrens, wildebeest herds, and wolf packs (Kershenbaum 2020, 170). To add an entertaining frisson of fringe scientific speculation to the proceedings, though, *Mass Effect* builds into its lore that the asari procreate through parthenogenesis, or the production of offspring from copied, unfertilized eggs, which also eliminates the need for certain competitive aspects of sexual selection. This biological alterity explains why the asari are flummoxed and bemused by norms of gender and sexuality that dominate human and other alien cultures.[4]

The scientifically precise distinctiveness of alien species in the *Mass Effect* series suggests the general astrobiological principle that species emerge by adapting to environmental conditions, which entails both the possibility of convergent evolution, where analogous but distant ecological niches produce sameness in biological structures, and the likelihood of biodiversity on alien planets being radically divergent from life observable on Earth. Moreover, puzzling out abstract and expositional scientific knowledge from the concrete context of implicit narrative world-building is built into actively exploring the open worlds of *Mass Effect*. Hence a player may overhear a customer at Zakera Café request both levo-based and dextro-based food spices to a nonplussed shopkeeper. In the Codex, the player may then learn that amino acids of the quarian and turian species have different chirality—a chemical term from the Greek for "hand"— meaning that a molecular object differs from its mirror image. Amino-acid molecules are tetrahedrons that indeed exhibit chirality; most polypeptide chains of amino acids that naturally occur on Earth have levo-based (or left-handed) configurations. However, a plausible but surprising astrobiological speculation is that aliens could have dextro-based (or right-handed) configurations. In actual biochemistry, the ingestion of dextro-formed molecules in levo-based humans makes limonene taste orange-flavored,

[4]This idea that the evolution of morality, emotional connection, and even religious or tribal communities is all connected to natural selection has been studied as "group selection" by contemporary biologists such as David Wilson. Likewise, the seminal scientist Lynn Margulis argued that evolution frequently works by a cooperative and interdependent "symbiogenesis" of a species and its environment, based on the analogy of eukaryotic mitochondria and chloroplasts, and their historical genesis of a new symbiotic species through the incorporation of invasive prokaryotic bacteria into new cellular functions.

and levo-formed molecules make limonene taste like lemons; likewise, the dextro-formed molecules make thalidomide cure morning sickness in pregnant women, but the levo-formed molecule can induce birth defects (Catling 2014, 38). It stands to reason, then, that if a turian or quarian ate spices with the wrong chirality for their species, they could possibly experience an allergic reaction; therefore, the shopkeeper is justifiably dubious of the customer's purchase of spices with different chirality.

This fascinating astrobiological speculation about physiological alterity depends on the assumption that chirality in terrestrial biochemistry is the product of random evolutionary permutations and recombinations. And indeed a popular theory about homochirality posits that it derives from a contingent quirk in how life originated from prebiotic mineral surfaces. The standard astrobiological speculation on divergent evolution then logically follows: what if the starting conditions for life were different on an alien world? Such informed hard SF speculation in *Mass Effect* is not always so subtly embedded in the background world-building, though. For instance, the series foregrounds the dramatic look of the thin, tall turians, who resemble a humanoid cross of a raptor and crocodile, and make for striking visuals: they have a jagged exoskeleton of a body, a rough carapace of shoulder bones, mandible-like mouths, and a horned crest on their heads. The codex explains that the hardiness of this bodily frame derives from the astronomical fact that the turian homeworld of Palavan has a weak magnetic field and therefore evolution favored protection from the relatively high doses of solar radiation the planet and its indigenous inhabitants regularly weather.

Another evocative speculation about alien physiologies that promotes both scientific literacy and transformative engagement with implications of the scientific worldview is the reptilian species called the drell. The drell are a sapient species that push the envelope for what counts as general intelligence, revealing the anthropocentric bias inherent in such conversations. For the drell are a sophisticated species capable of sudden flashes of total eidetic memory that manifest as hypnotic trances of sensory overload, depicted in the flashy cinematic cut-scenes of the game as rapid jump cuts accompanied by a stream-of-consciousness monologue steeped in vivid description, all of which disrupts the smooth flow of abstract and rational discourse. However, a core criterion of intelligence evident in species as varied as chimpanzees and octopuses is behavioral learning, or the capacity to apply ingrained memories to new environmental challenges. Naturally, then, the Codex of *Mass Effect* frames the eidetic memory of the drell as deriving from the arid environment of their homeworld, Kahje, and the need to observe, learn, and recall the location of vegetation, drinkable water, and prey migration paths across immense stretches of desiccated land.[5]

Xenobiological theorists also frequently speculate on general intelligence as being bound up with numeracy and the capacity for apprehending abstract mathematical concepts. The amphibious salarians were able to preserve the lush jungle habitats of their homeworld, Sur'Kesh, due to their gifts for numeracy and their devotion to ecologically sustainable scientific and technological development. Mordin Solus, the cerebral salarian scientist that Shepard recruits for the Normandy, speaks in an overwhelming barrage of sentence fragments as he continually quantizes the data of his immediate environment. Yet in an implicit rebuke of the gap between mathematically precise scientific theory and its unintended applications in the real world, Mordin's overarching narrative arc in the series involves his confrontation with his former student, Maelon Heplorn, who is disillusioned with the hubris of his science-worshiping species who take it upon themselves to eugenically "play god". Maelon therefore conducts verboten research to reverse the sterilizing genophage that the salarians invented and that plunged the krogans into an extinction vortex. Assuming Mordin survives the suicide mission and the player as Shepard chooses to preserve Maelon's data, Mordin will be forever changed by his former student's critique and eventually make a heroically successful attempt—in a valiant act of self-sacrifice given Reaper resistance—to cure the genophage by repurposing a space elevator on Tuchanka called the Shroud into a global aerosol.

As a final wrinkle that calls into the question whether truly alien astrobiology and exoplanets can ever be totally scientifically knowable, it is tempting to interpret Mordin's genophage cure and heroic techno-fix (to

---

[5] This chapter has only brushed the surface of astrobiological speculation in the *Mass Effect* series, touching on some exemplary cases to illustrate some fundamental principles of the scientific speculation that drive the cognitive estrangement. There are myriad other examples of interesting speculation about uncanny alien physiologies in the videogames, including the following: the reptilian krogans who demonstrate scaling laws of body type and dominance hierarchies; the elephantine elcor who verbally tag their speech intonation since they cannot convey tone through their vocal apparatus, even though they are keenly emotionally intelligent about pheromones; and the jellyfish-like hanar and the Lovecraftian leviathans, which not only vividly show the probable necessity of liquid water in the origins of interstellar alien life, but also are unique variations on the ever-popular SF trope of the Fortean bladder.

correct a previously botched techno-fix) in light of the overall ambivalent treatment of numeracy as a potential characteristic of intelligent alien life, and the overall nuanced way the videogame entertainment undermines the heavy-handed transmission model of science communication endemic to earlier eras of pedagogical space opera. What makes *Mass Effect* so engagingly refreshing, and therefore effective as science communication, after all, is the way the game embeds scientific anxieties and pleasures into the ludic playground of a vastly interactive narrative and deeply immersive gameplay. The ambivalent portrayal of science in the series encourages players not just to passively receive streams of scientific data but to actively help construct and participate in critical and engaged public attitudes toward scientific discourse.

Take, for a final example, a minor incident that occurs in the Citadel mission, which was a narrative of extra downloadable content released after *Mass Effect 3* and especially beloved by fans for all its inside jokes, ironic meta-tributes, and wry self-commentary. Sandwiched between the end of the *Mass Effect* original series and the beginning of the final universe-changing mission, the immensely enjoyable narrative revolves around a shore-leave reunion bash interrupted by a kidnapping plot orchestrated by an evil Shepard clone. Indeed, the small masterpiece of a story serves as witty, action-packed coda and clever send up of all the narrative and gameplay gradually accrued over the preceding three gargantuan games. Featuring possible cameos by (or memorials for) all of the major characters of the series, the story allows Shepard, while preparing for the party in Admiral Anderson's luxurious apartment, to listen to an audio recording of a Mordin Solus, who is now possibly deceased, and his appearance on the educational program "Science Fun Today".

In the program, Mordin tells the child-age audience that science "education" is "vital for future" but cautions it "can seem esoteric, indirect". For the purposes of a demonstration of how to neutralize dangerous predators with common household chemicals, Mordin then abruptly releases an alien animal called a varen onto the set, before realizing that the children's puppet, Perry, is designed to look like a pyjak, an alien space-monkey and prey species to the varen. From Mordin's clipped audio commentary, it seems that the varen then attacks one of the children, and Mordin suggests the child "go limp" before realizing that the varen is instead only attempting to mate. Mordin drily adds, "see, children, the key to science is testing hypothesis, making observations", before concluding, "next hypothesis attempt neural shock". This darkly amusing incident reenacts in microcosm the egregious ethical failures of salarian science while probing the way the transmission of the scientific worldview is cloaked under the mantle of benign science education. The found recording therefore serves both as a fittingly ironic post-script to Mordin's narrative arc and a meaningful illustration of the way *Mass Effect* as a series both acclimates players to and performatively transgresses the known boundaries of exoplanetary and astrobiological science.

REFERENCES

BioWare. 2007. *Mass Effect 1*. BioWare. PC/Mac/Consoles.
———. 2010. *Mass Effect 2*. BioWare. PC/Mac/Consoles.
———. 2012. *Mass Effect 3*. BioWare. PC/Mac/Consoles.
———. 2021. *Mass Effect: Legendary Edition*. BioWare. PC/Mac/Consoles.
Carroll, Sean. 2007. *Dark Matter, Dark Energy: The Dark Side of the Universe*. Chantilly: The Teaching Company.
Catling, David. 2014. *Astrobiology: A Very Short Introduction*. Oxford: Oxford University Press.
Greenemeier, Larry. 2010. Video Game Expands the Concept of Dark Energy for *Mass Effect*. *Scientific American*, January 25. www.scientificamerican.com/article/dark-energy-mass-effect
Kershenbaum, Arik. 2020. *The Zoologist's Guide to the Galaxy: What Animals on Earth Reveal About Aliens and Ourselves*. New York: Penguin Random House.
Markley, Robert. 2005. *Dying Planet: Mars in Science and the Imagination*. Durham: Duke University Press.
Milburn, Colin. 2015. *Mondo Nano: Fun and Games in the World of Digital Matter*. Durham: Duke University Press.
Mitchell, Sara. 2012. Exploring the Galaxy with *Mass Effect 3*. *Blueshift*, July 31. https://asd.gsfc.nasa.gov/blueshift/index.php/2012/07/31/explorin-the-galaxy-with-mass-effect-3
Murray, Janet H. 1997. *Hamlet on the Holodeck: The Future of Narrative in Cyberspace*. New York: The Free Press.
Tasker, Elizabeth. 2017. *The Planet Factory: Exoplanets and the Search for a Second Earth*. London: Bloomsbury Sigma.
Tringham, Neal. 2015. *Science Fiction Video Games*. Boca Raton: CRC Press.
Westfahl, Gary. 2007. *Hugo Gernsback and the Century of Science Fiction*. Jefferson: McFarland.

CHAPTER 6

Conclusion

Although the dialogue-wheel and interrupt mechanics that allow players to select options that result in significant narrative branching have become common practice in both high-profile and indie narrative-based games, the *Mass Effect* series still stands out for the sheer copiousness with which such meaningful player choices shape the gradually unfolding long-form narrative. The original cross-pollination of genre-SF tropes and idioms with innovative videogame mechanics and affordances likewise can be glimpsed in a number of remarkable videogames productions since the release of the original *Mass Effect* series—the recent high-profile and award-winning *Dishonored 2* (2016), *The Outer Worlds* (2019), *Control* (2019), and *The Last of Us: Part II* (2020) immediately come to mind. However, the rapturous attention that the 2021 remastered Legendary edition of the original *Mass Effect* trilogy received in the popular media and among the gaming community testifies to the fact that the series still represents a highwater mark of videogame space opera. The lingering controversy over the ending of *Mass Effect 3* underscores the extent to which meaningful player agency is greatly valued in new collaboratively authored, interactive media. The controversy also suggests that those who nurture untenable notions of singular identifications with fictional characters will eventually have to rework their underlying assumptions given this imminent future of SF videogames in which narrow notions of how sophisticated narrative-driven videogames work will be sorely tried.

© The Author(s), under exclusive license to Springer Nature   85
Switzerland AG 2023
J. Winter, *BioWare's Mass Effect*, Palgrave Science Fiction and
Fantasy: A New Canon,
https://doi.org/10.1007/978-3-031-18876-3_6

A series like *Mass Effect* throws down the gauntlet to gamers, designers, critics, and scholars to attend to the ludonarrative means by which character customization, level design, open worlds, and interactions with artificially intelligent non-player characters crystallize into allegories for our social and historical context. The widescreen baroque of space opera has a rich tradition of vividly portraying the tangled intersections of diplomatic realpolitik and the legacy of colonialist and capitalist technological progress in fabulously imagined future scenarios. More concentrated study is therefore needed for how role-playing adventures have harnessed these genre-SF conventions to the specific protocols and affordances of the videogame medium. The tendency to categorically dismiss all popular space-opera entertainments as naïve, escapist fantasy is as prevalent today as is the inclination to blanketly censor all shooter videogames as legitimating state-authorized and antisocial violence. Given the routine condemnations of both videogames and space opera as ideological, oneiric, and depthless forms of popular culture, the complex artistry of a videogame series like *Mass Effect* has only begun to be genuinely assessed or appreciated on a wider cultural level.

One diverse audience that has already warmly recognized the achievement of the original *Mass Effect* trilogy, however, are feminist, nonwhite, and LBTQ gamers. Further scholarly study of the original series for the intersection of gender, sexuality, and race with topics not discussed in this book but abundantly represented in the games—such as disability, visuality, post-secular religion, animal studies, or indigeneity—would doubtless be richly rewarding. It is non-controversial to state that big-budget videogames today are on average more inclusive and diverse in their representations of nonwhite, queer, and female characters, players, and audiences than they were even just ten years ago; and LGBT romances have likewise proliferated in recent years. Yet the original *Mass Effect* series is still a distinctly memorable benchmark for the explicitness and nuance that it brought to the romance gameplay mechanic and for its long-form narrative commitment to a pluralistic, non-xenophobic future. Given the recent Gamergate controversy, to witness videogame culture extend such initial modest efforts for radical inclusion beyond the limited domain of what was boundary-pushing a mere decade ago would constitute an urgently needed step forward.

The rigorous attention to scientific verisimilitude in a big-budget, deeply customizable entertainment like the *Mass Effect* series suggests one vital means by which the seemingly widening gulf between science and the public can be bridged. The so-called gamification of science—especially in the actual peer-reviewed research of "citizen-science" games—has only begun to be formally studied; and hopefully the deep integration of scientific communities with a curious and resourceful groundswell of laypeople and nonexperts awaits its full implementation in future popular entertainments and culture at large. In an era shaped by post-truth disinformation campaigns against undeniable realities as varied as vaccinations and climate change, the onus is on scientific professionals as much as the general public to break down the arbitrary barriers of hostility and antagonism that blockade scientific research from its widest possible dissemination. An immensely popular game series such as *Mass Effect* offers a provocative case study for increasing participation in scientific discourse in a fashion that does not condescend to, bore, or imperiously exclude its eager, intelligent mass audience.

As a recently invented intellectual property in a marketplace dominated by legacy reboots and franchise crossovers, it will be fascinating to witness how the future of the series departs from, morphs, and expands on the precedent set by the original *Mass Effect* trilogy, including what happens with the planned sequels and transmedia adaptations in development. Regardless of that as-yet-undetermined prospect, videogames and the SF genre will surely continue to cross-pollinate and develop in tandem in the coming years, perpetually restyling the astonishing multiplicity of established SF memes and icons familiar to increasingly genre-savvy audiences. As extensively discussed in this book, these exciting story-rich elements promise to be refashioned by some of the following design affordances tailored to the peculiar immersions and interactivity of the videogame medium, such as narrative choice, long-form role-playing adventure, avatar customization, romance interactions, level and gameplay structure, a nonlinear interactive codex, open-world exploration, and science simulation. The sheer artistic triumph of the original *Mass Effect* trilogy, not to mention its endlessly renewable storehouse of just plain fun, stems from its masterful and creative synthesizing of videogame design and SF genre materials. Yet the intricate narrative blueprints of the evolving canon of SF literature and media have only begun to be excavated, re-engineered, and transmuted into a new canon of thrilling masterworks.

Bibliography of Scholarship on the *Mass Effect* Series

Bissell, Tom. 2010. Mass Effects. In *Extra Lives: Why Videogames Matter*, 105–128. New York: Pantheon Books.

Bosman, Frank. 2017. There is No Solution! "Wicked Problems" in Digital Games. *Games and Culture* 14 (5): 543–559.

Boyan, Andy, Matthew Grizzard, and Nicholas David Bowman. 2015. A Massively Moral Game? Mass Effect as a Case Study to Understand the Influence of Player's Moral Intuitions on Adherence to Hero or Antihero Play Styles. *Journal of Gaming and Virtual Worlds* 7 (1): 41–57.

Callahan, David. 2019. Don't Fear the Reapers, Fear Multiculturalism: Canadian Contexts and Ethnic Elisions in *Mass Effect*. *The International Journal of Computer Game Research* 19 (2), October 2019.

Carvalho, Marino. 2015. Leaving Earth, Preserving History: Uses of the Future in the *Mass Effect* Series. *Games and Culture* 10 (2): 127–148.

Clough, Michelle. 2017. Sexualization, Shirtlessness, and Smoldering Gazes: Desire and the Male Characters. In *Digital Love: Romance and Sexuality in Video Games*, ed. Heidi McDonald, 3–36. New York: CRC Press.

Consalvo, Mia, Thorsten Busch, and Carolyn Jong. 2019. Playing a Better Me: How Players Rehearse Their Ethos via Moral Choices. *Games and Culture* 14 (3): 216–235.

Crowley, Adam. 2020. Shut Up and Get Over Here: Lovers and Cattle in *Mass Effect*. In *Women's Space: Essays on Female Characters in 21st Century Science Fiction Western*, ed. Melanie A. Marotta, 59–71. Jefferson, NC: McFarland.

Dodd, Julian. 2020. Blurred Lines: Ravasio on "Historically Informed Performance". *Journal of Aesthetics and Art Criticism* 78 (1): 85–89.

J. Winter, *BioWare's Mass Effect*, Palgrave Science Fiction and Fantasy: A New Canon,
https://doi.org/10.1007/978-3-031-18876-3

Dutton, Nathan, Mia Consalvo, and Todd Harper. 2011. Digital Pitchforks and Virtual Torches: Fan Responses to the Mass Effect News Debacle. *Convergence: The International Journal of Research into New Media Technologies* 17 (3): 287–305.

Frelik, Paweł. 2014. Video Games. In *The Oxford Handbook of Science Fiction*, ed. Rob Latham, 226–238. Oxford: Oxford University Press.

Fuchs, Michael, Vanessa Erat, and Stefan Rabitsch. 2018. Playing Serial Imperialists: The Failed Promises of BioWare's Video Game Adventures. *Journal of Popular Culture* 51 (6): 1476–1499.

Gonzalez, Maricruz. 2014. The "Shepard" Will Guide Us: A Textual Analysis of Hegemonic Reinforcement and Resistance in the *Mass Effect* Video Game Series. Thesis. Dorothy F. Schmidt College of Arts and Letters.

Green, Amy M. 2018. *Storytelling in Video Games (Studies in Gaming)*. Jefferson: McFarland.

Harper, Todd. 2017. Role-play as Queer Lens: How "ClosetShep" Changed my Vision of *Mass Effect*. In *Queer Game Studies*, ed. B. Ruberg and A. Shaw, 125–134. Minneapolis: University of Minnesota Press.

Hayden, Craig. 2017. The Procedural Rhetorics of Mass Effect: Video Games as Argumentation in International Relations. *International Studies Perspectives* 18 (2): 175–193.

Jørgensen, Kristine. 2010. Game Characters as Narrative Devices: A Comparative Analysis of *Dragon Age: Origins* and *Mass Effect 2*. *Eludamos, Journal for Computer Game Culture* 4 (2): 315–331.

Krampe, Theresa. 2018. No Straight Answers: Queering Hegemonic Masculinity in BioWare's *Mass Effect*. *Game Studies* 18 (2).

Krobová, Tereza, Ondřej Moravec, and Jaroslav Švelch. 2015. Dressing Commander Shepard in Pink: Queer Playing in a Heteronormative Game Culture. *Cyberpsychology: Journal of Psychosocial Research on Cyberspace* 9 (3).

Kuling, Peter. 2014. Outing Ourselves in Outer Space: Canadian Identity Performances in BioWare's Mass Effect Trilogy. *Canadian Theatre Review* 159: 43–47.

Lavigne, Carlen. 2015. "She's a Soldier, not a Model": Feminism, FemShep and the *Mass Effect 3* Vote. *Journal of Gaming & Virtual Worlds* 7 (3): 317–329.

Lucas, Alexandra. 2017. From Smoldering Justicar to Blue-Skinned Space Babe: Asari Sexuality in Mass Effect. In *Digital Love: Romance and Sexuality in Videogames*, ed. Heidi McDonald, 69–76. New York: CRC Press.

Murzyn, Eva, and Evelien Valgaren. 2016. Our Virtual Selves, Our Virtual Morals: Mass Effect Players' Personality and In-Game Choices. In *2016 International Conference on Interactive Technologies and Games*. The Institute of Electrical and Electronics Engineers, Inc.

Patterson, Christopher B. 2014. Role-Playing the Multiculturalist Umpire: Loyalty and War in BioWare's Mass Effect Series. *Games and Culture* 10 (3): 207–228.

Phillips, Amanda. 2020. Does Anyone Really Identify with FemShep? Troubling Identity (and) Politics in *Mass Effect*. In *Gamer Trouble: Feminist Confrontations in Digital Culture*. New York: New York University Press.

Reardon, Daniel, David Wright, and Edward A. Malone. 2016. Quest for the Happy Ending to Mass Effect 3: The Challenges of Cocreation with Consumers in a post-Certeauian Age. *Technical Communication Quarterly* 26 (1): 42–58.

Ricksand, Martin. 2020. Walton, Truth in Fiction, and Video Games: A Rejoinder to Willis. *Journal of Aesthetics and Art Criticism* 78 (1): 101–104.

Sohovnen, Tanja. 2020. Game Characters as Tools of Expression: Modding the Body in Mass Effect. In *Women and Videogame Modding: Essays on Gender and Digital Community*, ed. Bridget Whelan. Jefferson: McFarland.

Tomlinson, Christine. 2019. Gaming on Romance. *Contexts* 18 (4): 50–52.

Travis, Roger. 2012. Epic Style: Re-Compositional Performance in the BioWare Digital RPGs. In *Dungeons, Dragons, and Digital Denizens*, ed. Gerald Voorhees, Joshua Call, and Katie Whitlock, 219–234. New York: Continuum International Publishing Group.

Voorhees, Gerald. 2012. Neo-liberal Multiculturalism in Mass Effect: The Government of Difference in Digital RPGs. In *Dungeons, Dragons, and Digital Denizens*, ed. Gerald Voorhees, Joshua Call, and Katie Whitlock, 259–277. New York: Continuum International Publishing Group.

Willis, Marissa. 2019. Choose Your Own Adventure: Examining the Fictional Content of Video Games as interactive Fictions. *The Journal of Aesthetics and Art Criticism* 77 (1): 43–53.

Zakowski, Samuel. 2014. Time and Temporality in the *Mass Effect* Series: A Narratological Approach. *Games and Culture* 9 (1): 58–79.

Zekany, Eva. 2016. "A Horrible Interspecies Awkwardness Thing": (Non)Human Desire in the *Mass Effect* Universe. *Bulletin of Science, Technology, and Society* 36 (1): 67–77.

INDEX[1]

---

[1] Note: Page numbers followed by 'n' refer to notes.